MW01006022

IMPRIMI POTEST

Romae, die 18 decembris 2003

R.P. Francisco J. Egaña, S.J.
Vice-Rector Universitatis

IMPRIMATUR

Dal Vicariato di Roma, 12 gennaio 2004

Mons. Mauro Parmeggiani
Prelato Segretario Generale

ISBN 88-7652-982-9

Editrice Pontificia Università Gregoriana
Piazza della Pilotta, 35 - 00187 Roma, Italia

Contents

in mind he enrolled for a doctorate in philosophy at the University of Freiburg. At that time Martin Heidegger was lecturing in philosophy. But Rahner chose a Catholic professor, Martin Honecker as his mentor. Rahner obviously followed lectures of Heidegger but he has denied that Heidegger was an important influence upon him. His own studies were in St. Thomas but Rahner pursued an interpretation of Thomas that was inspired by the Belgian Jesuit philosopher, Marechal. In the end Honecker rejected Rahner's thesis as too daring. But we shouldn't assume that Rahner had a crisis over this. In fact he had already shifted gears and had enrolled to do a doctorate in theology in Innsbruck under instruction of the Jesuit superiors. It seems that they had changed their plans for him, destining him to teach theology. By this time, Karl's brother Hugo was Rector of the University and perhaps he played a role in bringing Karl to Innsbruck.

After the war Karl pursued a typical academic career. First he was professor of theology at Innsbruck. These were creative years in which Rahner developed an original approach to many classical theological problems. His key insight was to begin with the human being whom Rahner saw as characterized by transcendence, an ever greater openness to God. Rahner situated the great theological issues around human transcendence. He was brought to the Second Vatican Council by Cardinal Koenig as an expert. Here Rahner influenced a number of counciliar texts such as Dei Verbum, the Constitution on Divine Revelation. After the Council Rahner was professor for a few years in Munich where he followed Romano Guardini in lecturing on the Christian world-view. Rahner didn't have great success in this chair. Guardini was famous for his literary and poetical style. Rahner, on the other hand, was dense and abstract, and strictly speaking his chair wasn't in theology as such. So Rahner accepted a chair of theology in the University of Munster. Here he developed his creative and genial synthesis of the faith called <u>Foundations of Christian Faith</u>.

After his retirement in 1971 Rahner continued to be active writing and lecturing on a host of diverse theological themes. He never ceased to be interested in new questions. He never closed in upon himself but remained creative and open until the end. He died shortly after his 80th birthday in 1984.[1]

Theologian of the Spirit

The focus of our study in this book is Rahner's spirituality. I want to argue that offering a Christian spirituality is the key to Rahner's theology. He was a brilliant speculative thinker and we will touch upon some of his key ideas. But I argue that Rahner's theological reflections were always ordered to living the Christian faith. Indeed I want to argue that his key theological insights revolve around the intuition that all men and women have the capacity to have an experience of God, indeed an immediate experience

---

[1] Rahner's formidable intellect led his Jesuit brothers to hold him in awe. But essentially he was a shy man. In his final years, with the help of his secretary, Rahner was often taken for drives in the country by his Jesuit students. Rahner was delighted with these contacts which his shyness prevented him from requesting.

ence, which naturally have their own characteristics both personal and historical; I am not going to talk about forms and visions, symbols, voices, tears and such things. All I say is I knew God, nameless and unfathomable, silent and yet near, bestowing himself upon me in his Trinity, I knew God beyond all concrete imaginings. I knew him clearly in such nearness and grace as is impossible to confound or mistake."[3]

Just a few observations on this remarkable passage may help us to grasp the import of what Rahner is saying here. Obviously God is the Infinite God, the God beyond the world, the God who cannot be identified with any objects in the world, God the Trinity. But secondly this God can be known immediately by grace. In the pages which follow we shall have to plumb what Rahner means by this term grace. Third Rahner says that his experience of God which is immediate is not that of visions. Hence in this sense it is not extraordinary. So Rahner is arguing that an experience of God is not reserved for the few, for those with special psychic gifts or even for those endowed with special revelations or divine touches. Rather the Infinite God draws near and is available to all in their everyday life.

An Answer to our Question

Rahner's companion and critic, the theologian Hans Urs von Balthasar, bitterly lamented the separation that has taken place in recent centuries between theology

---

[3] "Ignatius of Loyola Speaks to a Modern Jesuit," in Ignatius of Loyola edited by Paul Imhof (London: Collins, 1979), p. 11.

and spirituality. If the great Fathers of the Church were both theologians and masters of the Spirit, in modern times theologians have not always been or perhaps even often noted for their holiness or spiritual insights. Especially in the heyday of scholasticism[4], theology became dry and abstract. But in Rahner we have once again a theology which grows out of his basic spiritual intuition derived from St. Ignatius Loyola, that it is possible to have an experience of God and indeed to find God in everything. In this sense I believe it is worth the effort to seek to understand his theology, for as he himself said, it was written to enable contemporary men and women to believe with integrity, and not only to believe, but also to surrender to the Mystery without whom life can only be trivial.

For Furthering Reading:

Karl Rahner, "Ignatius of Loyola Speaks to a Modern Jesuit," in Ignatius of Loyola edited by Paul Imhof, London, 1979, pp. 11-38.

Hans Urs von Balthasar, "Theology and Sanctity," in Explorations in Theology 1: The Word Made Flesh, San Francisco, 1989, pp. 181-209.

---

[4] The scholastic method was that of question and answer, with an eye to possible objections to theological positions. This method was employed in the High Middle Ages. In the era before the Second Vatican Council, this method was often pursued in Catholic faculties of theology, often developing with ever great subtlety the responses of the great scholastic thinkers like Aquinas and Suarez.

CHAPTER TWO

God

"What a poor creature you have made me, O God, All I know about You and about myself is that You are the eternal mystery of my life. Lord, what a frightful puzzle man is! He belongs to you, and You are the Incomprehensible—Incomprehensible in your Being and even more so in Your ways and judgments...But if You were not incomprehensible, You would be inferior to me, for my mind could grasp and assimilate You. You would belong to me, instead of I to You. And that would truly be hell, if I should belong only to myself! It would be the fate of the damned, to be doomed to pace up and down for all eternity in the cramped and confining prison of my own finiteness."

<u>Encounters with Silence</u>

St. Thomas Aquinas says that the object of theology is God. Whatever is examined in theology must be done with reference to God. If this rule is not always observed by many theologians, it is pre-eminently the guiding motif of Rahner's theology.

Rahner notes that the word 'God' is a strange word. If other words such as book, tree, rock point to things in this world, the word God does not have an obvious reference point. God is beyond the world. Indeed if we could point to some object and call it God, that would be a contradiction in terms. For objects are by their very nature finite whereas God is infinite.

Still the word 'God' exists. We find this word in human language. What role does this word God play in human discourse? Rahner says that the word God points to the totality of reality. Without this word the human being would be nothing more than fragmentariness. Rahner argues that the word God allows the human being to see himself as a totality. He writes: without this word, "Man would forget all about himself in his preoccupation with all the individual details of his world and his existence. He would never face the totality of the world and of himself, helplessly, silently, anxiously…He would have forgotten the totality and its ground, and at the same time, if we can put it this way, would have forgotten that he had forgotten."[1] If this could happen, Rahner argues the human being would no longer be a human being. He would be nothing more than a clever animal. Let us see why Rahner holds this.

As we have already seen, the key to human existence is transcendence, that is the human being is not limited to any object in this world. As soon as he knows or chooses an object in the world, he sees that the object is limited and cannot fulfill him absolutely. He transcends all objects in a dynamic movement toward God.

Rahner is influenced by St. Thomas's idea that the human being has two faculties, intellect and will. Using more contemporary terminology, Rahner speaks of knowledge and freedom. For Rahner, all knowing involves three dimensions. First, I know

[1] Karl Rahner, *Foundations of Christian Faith* (London: Darton, Longman and Todd, 1978), p. 48.

something. There is an objective dimension to knowing. But secondly, when I know something in the world, at the same time I know mysef. I may be not explicitly reflecting about this. But my knowledge of myself as subject is co-present whenever I know objects. But Rahner goes further. Since in every act of knowing an object, I transcend that object, it follows that in every act of knowldege I know God. God is the final goal or horizon of all my knowing. No object can ever satisfy my hunger to know. Each object propels me ahead. Implicitly I am finding God as the goal of my transcendence. God pulls me beyond all limited objects to his infinite fullness.[2]

Rahner makes a parallel analysis for human freedom. As a subject I have freedom of choice. I have an infinite range of objects of choice. But more importantly, in choosing objects I am choosing myself. I am making myself through my free choices. These choices may be banal in some cases, for example, what clothes I put on on a given day. But many choices are radically significant, for example the choice of a career or a spouse. So in all freedom there is an objective and subjective dimension. I chose objects and I choose myself. But once again Rahner argues that the goal of human freedom is God. In choosing objects I realize that they are limited. They cannot fulfill me. Recognizing their limited character, I already transcend them. Only God can completely satisfy the

---

[2] Rahner argues that the ultimate goal cannot be an object, because an object will always be transcended, neither can the goal be nothing, for nothing grounds nothing. Nothing cannot be the source of human transcendence.

dynamism of my human freedom. When Rahner says this, he is taking up the classical theme of freedom as we find it in St. Augustine. "Our hearts are restless and they shall not rest until they rest in thee."

Two points here call for attention. One is that on this understanding God is the ground of all human freedom. God doesn't oppose human freedom but makes it possible. If there were no God, the human being wouldn't be free. He would be determined to some object. But precisely because God exists, human beings transcend all worldly realities. Secondly, in this context it is clear in what idolatry consists. If I limit myself to some object whether it be money, career, fame, beauty, sex, I turn into an idolater. I give myself without reserve to an object, whereas I am called to an ever greater openness to God. Only God can fulfill my liberty. In fact freedom means an openness to surrender to the God ever greater.

In this context we can understand something of Rahner's preferred language for God.

Since the word God carries a lot of baggage for many people, Rahner prefers to use the word Mystery. In fact he often refers to God as Holy Mystery. The term mystery indicates that God exceeds all our powers of comprehending and grasping, not because God is not intelligible but because his is a fullness of intelligibility which exceeds all our concepts. The phrase evokes something of classical Greek Christian theology which sees God as dazzling darkness. Referring to God as Holy Mystery, Rahner wants to emphasize that God is the ground and goal of our freedom. Since God is holy, we are entitled to surrender to him. Rahner regularly employs a number of adjectives when talking about

God. God is anonymous, for example, meaning that God is beyond all names. God is unavailable in the sense that God exceeds all our attempts to master him. God can also be said to be indefnible and ineffable. At times Rahner also refers to God as an infinite Abyss.

For Rahner the key question of human existence is whether the human being can remain open to this Mystery or Abyss or whether he chooses to close himself in and dedicate himself solely to objects. Equally urgent for Rahner is whether one can trust this all-encompassing Mystery who is beyond our grasp. He finds the ultimate source for such trust in Christ who surrendered to God throughout his life, even in the darkest moment of the cross. We will come back to this aspect later. Here, however, it is important to say that for Rahner the key to human existence lies ultimately in freedom rather than in knowledge. In the last analysis if we are going to find fulfillment as human beings we need to do so by surrendering ourselves to the God whom we cannot control with our intelligence, the God to whom we must relate by surrendering ourselves in trust.

One final clarification. From what we have explained, it is obvious that human beings are constituted as religious beings. God belongs inescapably to human experience. At the time of the Enlightenment, some philosophers such as Feuerbach spoke of human beings creating God. But from the analysis which Rahner offers, the opposite is the case. It is God who allows us to be human beings. He writes, "We should not think that, because the phonetic sound of the word 'God' is always dependent on us, therefore the word 'God' is also our creation. Rather it creates us because it makes us men."[3] Hence without God as our ultimate horizon, we could not be human beings. If this is the case, a dramatic conclusion follows. The death of God would mean literally the death of human beings.

In the context of what we have presented here, I think it is legitimate to speak of Rahner as a mystical theologian. The term mysticism naturally has many different meanings.[4] In the tradition it often indicated experiences that went beyond the normal experiences of prayer. In some cases mysticism was identified with intense emotional experiences of God, the so-called mystical marriage experienced by saints like Teresa of Avila. At other times mysticism inicated extraordinary experiences of divine darkness. One can think of writers such as Meister Eckhart. In the tradition normally these experiences were seen as priveleges reserved for the few. I would justify the term mystical, first because Rahner stresses the dazzling darkness of God whom he refers to precisely as Mystery. In this sense Rahner stands in the apophatic tradition where God is experienced as beyond all imaginings. Before the Infinite God one can only stand in an attitude of speechless wonder. One is literally in apophasis: that is, speechless.

But Rahner differs from the mystical tradition in that he argues that the experience of God is not reserved for the few. Rather every man and woman is summoned to become a mystic. All of us are called to surrender ourselves to God, a surrender which nec-

---

[3] Op. cit., p. 50.
[4] See chapter one to Harvey Egan's <u>Christian Mysticism</u> (New York, 1984), pp. 1-29.

essarily takes place in darkness. But Rahner stresses as well that this mysticism takes place in everyday life. We live in this world, we play out our human existence immersed in the creation given us by God, but in the midst of all this, we know that no object is God. As Augustine says, each creature cries out, we have not made ouirselves. So in the midst of this world, we also flee from the world, in the sense that we surrender to the God beyond the world, the God always greater. But as we shall see in the chapters ahead, the God who is beyond the world will also summon us back to the world, for this Infinite God did not hesitate to become incarnate within the world.

For Further Reading:

Karl Rahner, <u>Foundations of Christian Faith</u>, London, 1978, pp. 44-51.

Karl Rahner, "The Human Question of Meaning in Face of the Absolute Mystery of God," <u>Theological Investigations</u> 18, London, 1984, pp. 89-104.

CHAPTER THREE

Grace as God's Self-Gift

We have already seen that as transcendence the human being has an immediate experience of God. He is referred to God in every act of knowing or choosing. Naturally this presence of God is given through the experience of objects in the world. So paradoxically, to use Rahner's language, it is an experience of mediated immediacy. Still, in this experience of God, God is lived as the ultimate Mystery of our lives, a Mystery who is nameless and silent. We do not know if God wishes to draw near to us.

This is where the Christian revelation enters in. All of Rahner's theology revolves around the idea that God wishes to give Himself to us as gift. This, according to Rahner, is the central message of the gospel. The Second Vatican Council stressed the universality of God's offer. In The Pastoral Constitution on the Church in the Modern world, we read: "By his Incarnation the Son of God united himself in some sense with every human being." The Constitution then goes on to speak of Christians being conformed to the likeness of Christ, receiving the Spirit of Christ and participating in his paschal mystery. The Constitution continues, "This applies not only to Christians but to all people of good will in whose hearts grace is secretly at work. Since Christ died for everyone, and since the ultimate calling of each of us comes from God and is therefore a universal one, we are obliged to hold that the Holy Spirit offers everyone the possibility of sharing in this paschal mystery in a manner known to God." (no. 22)

How does this take place? Rahner suggests that it is through the mystery of grace. Grace is one of the key words in the history of theology but a word which is often obscure. Very often, I think, the ordinary Christian thinks of grace as a thing. One wants to get grace and accumulate it as money in a bank account. Rahner prefers to think of grace as the immediate indwelling of God in the human person. Rahner's approach is rooted in the ancient Greek Christian theology of human divinization or deification through the indwelling of the Holy Spirit. In the theology of the Middle Ages St Thomas spoke about uncreated grace and created grace. For Thomas uncreated grace was the Holy Spirit. Thomas taught that God does not dwell directly in the soul. He taught this because he wanted to preserve the transcendence of God. Rather for Thomas, uncreated grace produced created grace, which was given to the soul enabling the soul to perform the supernatural acts of faith, hope and love.

For the most part Rahner focuses on uncreated grace or the presence of the Holy Spirit in the believer. He affirms that the Christian becomes the event of a loving self-communication of God. Rahner conceives of grace as an event. An event takes place, it is a happening, it is historical. With this accent on event, Rahner wants to stress that grace is a free gift of God. God was under no obligation to give himself

22

as gift. In this sense grace is supernatural, that is, in no way owed to the creature. Still, the fact that grace is free, does not mean that it is restricted to some. By our faith we know that God wishes all to be saved.[1] So even though grace is free it is offered to all. Of course we do not know if all accept grace. In this context it is clear that Rahner is hopeful for humankind but he doesn't affirm that all are saved in fact nor that it is impossible to reject God. But he does put the accent on God's universal offer.

In order to explain the free character of God's grace and its universal presence in human experience, Rahner coined a term called the supernatural existential.[2] In part he borrowed the language from the philosopher Martin Heidegger. Heidegger taught that in every human being there were certain inalienable structures. He referred to such a structure as an existential. An example would be temporality. It is impossible to be a human being without being in time. Rahner argued that human beings not only have natural existentials like temporality but also a supernatural one. This is the longing for God's presence, a longing to be in union with God. Rahner said that this longing is strictly supernatural. It exists in us because God freely planted it there. There is an emptiness in us which is there precisely because God wants to fill it. This is what Rahner meant by the supernatural existential.

[1] See, for example, 1 Tim. 2:4 "God desires that all be saved and come to the knowledge of the truth."

[2] To further clarify this point as well as to get a synthesis of Rahner's teaching on nature and grace, see, "Nature and Grace, in Theological Investigations 4 (London: Darton, Longman and Todd, 1966), pp. 165-188.

When God gives himself to us in grace, which is nothing other than his own self, there takes place a union of the human and the divine which is deeper than anything we can imagine. God and the human person become one. The human subject isn't absorbed into God nor does God cease to be transcendent but an indescribable union takes place. Rahner says that God becomes a co-constitutive dimension of human subjectivity. Obviously this cannot be explained, strictly speaking. One can only try to enter into the Mystery. But Rahner suggests that an analogy might help, that of formal causality. In Aristotelian philosophy, matter and form go together to make up a reality. For example, a statue is made of marble but it has the form of King David. These are inseparable. Something similar take place in the bestowal of grace. God becomes so much a part of me that my subjectivity is modified by God's presence. As Paul says, it is no longer I who live but Christ lives in me.

What Rahner is getting at here is very subtle. On the one hand the human person remains a human person. The person doesn't become God. The person remains an openness to God (transcendence) but now that openness to God is transformed by God's self-gift, by God's nearness. The horizon of transcendence is transformed. Human transcendence is lived under a new modality, that of God's closeness. It is according to human nature to be transcendence but according to God's self-gift, which is supernatural, transcendence has a new mode of being. Thus, in the concrete, nature never exists on its own, but only under the influence of grace. For Rahner, in fact, there is no such thing as a natural human being, for every human being is called to share God's life. God could have created a person without this vocation but in fact he has never done so. The only human being who exists is the creature under grace. Thus transcendence has two dimensions, one natural and the other supernatural. The natural dimension is the openness to God. The supernatural element is God's nearness and self-gift. These two are distinct but inseparable.

The upshot of all this is that Rahner can affirm that the human being has an immediate experience of God in a wholly new sense. If every act of knowing and loving is open to God, now Rahner can say that every human act is already transformed by God's self-gift. I can experience the nearness of God in everything. God can draw near to me in any act or circumstance of my life and when I respond to God's presence, my response is salvific, for my response is transformed by grace. This is what the theological tradition has called charity, that is, the response to God's self-offer by which God dwells in me. Because I have charity in my heart, I will be able to see God after death. Because I have charity, I can know God, since God is love (1 Jn. 4:16). Later we shall see that the ordinary way in which I respond to God's love in everyday life is through loving my neighbor. My response to God is through my response to my neighbor. As St. Ignatius says, charity is manifested in deeds (Spiritual Exercises, no. 230). So each day offers me an immediate experience of God, but once again a response mediated through creatures in the world, in this case, through my neighbor.

The whole thrust of Rahner's argument is that it is

always possible to experience God, that we are called to an immediate experience of God, in everyday life. At the same time Rahner doesn't deny that there are specially privileged moments where God's presence is felt more vividly. These experiences are not totally different from other experiences of God but they are heightened experiences of grace. Other theologians have spoken of disclosure experiences or signals of transcendence. Rahner thinks along the same lines arguing that there are privileged moments in which one has a heightened experience of grace. Examples would be: courage in the face of death, hope in a situation where there is no tangible motive for hope (for example in a concentration camp), love of another human being without any search for human compensation, fidelity to another without any reserve, willingness to forgive another gratuitously, an ultimate confidence and trust in the value and meaningfulness of human life, an implicit sense of being accepted, an intuition that reality is fundamentally gracious. In these and other similar experiences, human beings experience the gracious and loving reality of God in sheer immediacy.

For Further Reading:

Karl Rahner, "Reflections on the Experience of Grace, Theological Investigations 3, 1974, pp. 86-90.

Karl Rahner, "Man as the Event of God's Free and Forgiving Self-Communication," Foundations of Christian Faith, London, 1978, pp. 116-137.

CHAPTER FOUR

Karl Rahner and Ignatian Discernment

A central theme in our study of Rahner has been our theologian's insistence on the possibility of an immediate experience of God. In the last chapter I tried to show how Rahner's theology of grace underpins this conviction. In this chapter I want to explore this point further by relating Rahner's theology of grace to Ignatian discernment. I do this because Rahner says that he has been inspired by Ignatius and because, at least in one major study[1], he himself defends his position in the light of Ignatius's writings.

Let us first say a word about the Spiritual Exercises of St. Ignatius. Although they are often used to help people generally in their life in the Spirit, in fact Ignatius wrote them with a specific purpose, namely to help a person make a life decision, in other words, to help a person to discern God's will or to know where God is calling that person. So the Spiritual Exercises have as a goal to help a person to discover where God is acting in his or her life.

---

[1] "The Logic of Concrete Individual Knowledge in Ignatius Loyola," in The Dynamic Element in the Church (New York: Herder and Herder, 1964), pp. 84-170.

They are divided into four weeks or moments (hence not necessarily weeks in the temporal sense). In the first week the retreatant undergoes a type of conversion process, looking at God's plan for his creation and how sin mars God's work. The person tries to see how all that is happening concretely in his life. A person is then ready to enter the second week, where he or she seeks to follow Christ more closely. In the midst of the second week, the person seeks to find where God is calling him. He seeks to make his choice of a state of life. The life of Christ plays a key role in this. The exercitant seeks to find God's will by looking at Christ's life as a pattern for Christian living and as a source of the values by which he wishes to live. In principle the choice or the election is made in the second week. In the third and fourth week the retreatant prays the passion and resurrection of Christ. He uses these weeks to confirm the choice made. He asks God for the grace of illumination, to know whether indeed his choice already made is God's will. Part of the answer to the question lies in its conformity to the Easter mystery of Christ.

Let us look a bit more closely at the second week and the moment of election. Ignatius asks how I can know what God wants me to do. Ignatius assumes here that God does want something specific for each person. God has a project for each individual life. And this is something much more concrete than general moral values. Thus for example, it would be completely moral for me to choose married life or the life of a priest. But ethics as such cannot tell me what to choose. For this I have to make a discernment. Ignatius is convinced, and Rahner follows him in this, that in my prayer I can hear God's voice telling me how he is inviting me to follow him.

In the Spiritual Exercises Ignatius offers the retreatant so-called rules for discernment. He also notes that there are three times in which an election about a state of life can be made (see numbers 175, 176, 177). In the first time, the person knows without any doubt that God is directing him to a specific choice. In the second time, the person finds himself under the motion of different spirits in his soul. He at times finds himself in consolation, a sense of joy and peace and at other times in desolation, that is, turbulence of soul, agitation, discouragement etc. In the third time his soul is very calm. He neither has a clear conviction of what he should do nor does he undergo consolations and desolations.

In the first time, one doesn't have to make a discernment, for God's will is felt without doubt. In the third time, Ignatius suggests that one use one's reason. For example, one considers God's plan for his creatures and then reasons what would be a suitable means for me to use to cooperate with God's plan.

Both in giving the Spiritual Exercises and in theological reflection upon St. Ignatius, most attention is normally given to the use of consolation and desolation. First, let us say that by consolation Ignatius means a state where the soul feels completely inflamed with love of its Creator and Lord, so much so that it cannot love any creature on earth for its own sake but only for the sake of God the Lord (number 316). Note that Ignatius here doesn't say that we reject the world or creatures. Rather we love them in their appropriate context. They exist as mediators for the surrender of our lives to God.

Moreover, when distinguishing between consolation and desolation, we must note that the principal difference lies in whether these motions of the soul enable us to make greater acts of faith, hope and love or whether they block such virtues. We need to be subtle in looking at consolations and desolations. The immediate emotion can often be deceptive. It depends on the general condition of our soul, or in the terminology of the Spiritual Exercises, whether we find ourselves in the first week or the second week. For example, a person beginning the Exercises and in need of conversion, may be filled with repugnance at leading a moral life. The values of Christ might seem demanding even overwhelming. So he needs to resist sadness or discouragement. But the situation is different for a man in the second week. If his heart is firmly rooted in Christ, then he should normally experience peace and joy, the fruits which St. Paul associates with the Spirit (see Galatians 5:22-23). So in this case, consolation involves positive emotions whereas discouragement would be seen as the work of the evil spirit. One sees here that the trajectories of the first and second weeks are contrary. The type of delight experienced in the first week, for example in sensuality, is the work of the Evil One, whereas delight in the Second Week will be the work of the Holy Spirit.

In a short essay in America magazine[2], William Barry suggests that a fundamental rule of thumb is to

---

[2] See the issue for May 20, 2002, pp. 12-15.

look at the general orientation of our lives. If we are generally out of tune with God in our lives, then we can expect that God will try to get us to change our lives. Hence we will experience discomfort and pangs of conscience. On the other hand, if we are trying to live in tune with God's intention for us, then God will console us, help us to move forward, encourage us in our efforts to lead a good life. For example, if a landlord is gauging his tenants, increasing their rent unfairly and not providing them adequate services, when he tries to pray, he might very well find that God is pricking his conscience. This would be a sign of the Holy Spirit acting in his life. If on the other hand, a religious sister, who prays regularly and tries to live a life of service, is plagued by scruples about how faithful she is to her vows, there is good reason to think that this is the work of the evil spirit.

Ignatius makes the point, in the second week, that the evil spirit generally works by deceit, trying to lead us astray from God, by hiding this intention under the appearance of good. Ignatius himself had this experience in his devotion to the mass. He was so taken with God during the Eucharist, that he was flooded with tears and it took him several hours to celebrate mass. Through discernment, he came to see that this devotion was preventing him from a greater service to God by his apostolic work. From this moment of discernment, his devotion at mass was much more restricted.

Before turning to Rahner's interpretation of Ignatius, we should make one final point. In the Spiritual Exercises, St. Ignatius also speaks of so-called consolation without cause. In number 330, he writes, "God alone can give consolation to the soul without any previous cause. It belongs solely to the Creator to come into a soul, to leave it, to act upon it, to draw it wholly to the love of his Divine Majesty. I said without previous cause, that is, without any preceding perception or knowledge of any subject by which a soul might be led to such a consolation through its own acts of intellect and will."

Continuing this line of thought, Ignatius shows himself a good psychologist and observes that we have to be aware of the stages of a thought process. For example, I can be stirred up with love of God, and then in a secondary moment decide that therefore I will go as a missionary to the most desolate part of the world for the love of God. St. Ignatius says that the follow through is not necessarily the will of God. The beginning consolation without cause is a valid experience of God but it is possible that between the beginning and the end something has entered in, which is not directly from God. In other words the follow through of my original desire does not have God's guarantee. For example, I may have a serious medical condition that makes it absolutely foolish for me to think of working in an undeveloped part of the world. I would destroy myself and hence be of no use to others. Therefore no real love of God and neighbor.

As I say, Ignatius mentions this consolation without cause in the Spiritual Exercises. I should , however, mention one other place, for it is an important text in Ignatian studies and one to which Rahner specifically refers. It is a letter to Sr. Teresa Rajedella. There he writes, "It happens that often Our Lord moves and forces our soul to one way or another of acting by opening our soul; i.e. speaking inside it without any noise of voices, raising the whole of it to his divine love; with us not being able, even if we wanted, to resist his purpose;...Where quite often we can deceive ourselves is that, after the consolation or inbreathing of this kind, as the soul remains in delight, the enemy arrives."

How does Rahner interpret this traditional Ignatian material? First, he suggests that the three times for making an election should be understood in a descending order of importance. Thus Rahner gives priority to the first time. Secondly, he links this first time with the Ignatian idea of consolation without previous cause. Third, he interprets this consolation without previous cause in terms of his theology of grace. That is, he sees it in a transcendental way, as the human being's openness to God under the influence of the Holy Spirit. The fundamental human experience of God is thus the pure and radical being drawn to God without any other object. God Himself is the object of the human desire under grace and nothing blocks this dynamism. So Rahner interprets the 'without previous cause' not in a temporal sense, but in the sense of being objectless, that is, there is no object in this world which is the goal of this transcendence. Rather God himself is the goal. It is the being drawn to the God beyond all objects.

Rahner then comes to a discussion of consolations and desolations. Here he argues that we should interpret this second time in the light of the first. That is, in making a concrete choice, for example, of a state of life, we will look at our human affectivity. But fundamentally we are discerning whether these motions of the soul lead us in the direction of the consolation without cause as Rahner understands it, that is, are we being drawn in joy and peace to the ever greater God, the God beyond all things. In other words, in choosing something in this world, like a state of life, we are choosing a means for serving God. So what we want to do is to judge this choice over against the fundamental consolation. Does our choice foster this greater openness to God? We see if our choice leads to a synthesis in our lives between this objective choice and our openness to God. Does this objective choice express our dynamism to God without obstacles?

We might feel that this discussion of discernment is very complicated and is beyond the capabilities of the average Christian. But I think, as is so often the case with Rahner, his language and style of argument can deceive us and in fact he is saying something rather simple. When a person is confronted with an important choice in his life, his way of resolving it may be for the most part very intuitive. In his heart he bears some deep religious impulses. He will feel a desire to love God and to serve him generously. And in fact, rather intuitively, he will make his decision upon his instinct, as to whether this choice conforms to his basic religious convictions, to his higher desires. At times a person may do this more formally, in a prolonged experience of prayer or in a retreat, and no doubt Ignatius has many religious and psychological insights which will be of help. But discernment is probably another instance of a man knowing how to speak prose before he knows what prose is. In the sphere of finding God, a person will intuitively compare the choice which confronts him with his fundamental experience of being in love with God, an experience which both Ignatius and Rahner insist, is of itself infallible. So once again Rahner gives us a theological explanation of what he believes is the fundamental Christian experience.

Let me add a few critical reflections about Rahner's interpretation of St. Ignatius before concluding this chapter. First, one might naturally ask if Rahner is true to what Ignatius wrote. I don't think a simple answer to this question is possible. Some commentators[3], for example, don't believe that Ignatius prioritized the first time. Others don't agree with Rahner's linking together the first time and the consolation without cause. I would say that Rahner gives a creative interpretation of Ignatius which is valid in its own right. This is very typical of the philosophical and theological tradition. One reads Marechal's interpretation of St. Thomas or Heidegger's interpretation of Kant not for their historical value but for their own original contribution to thinking. The same can be said of Rahner's interpretation of Ignatius. It is a brilliant contribution to the discussion of how to find God in one's life.

Secondly, a number of commentators suggest that the gray area in Rahner's thought is with mediations. Rahner is consistent in showing the immediacy of the experience of God, an immediacy which he dares to call infallible, for God alone is the source of the

---

[3] See especially Philip Endean, Karl Rahner and Ignatian Spirituality (Oxford: Oxford University Press, 2001).

immediacy. Well and good. The difficulty, however, comes with the mediations of this immediacy. When we translate our joy in God into concrete action, we can be led astray. This could be as simple, for example, as a lack of information. A man chooses to become a Jesuit because he wants to be a teacher but then finds that Jesuits are meant to be available for many different kinds of mission. A man thinks he wants to marry this woman because she will be a good homemaker and only after the marriage discovers that she is deeply committed to realizing a career. Or perhaps, even more commonly, she discovers later in her life the importance to her of career. Or we can think of all the many unconscious psychological motivations which may influence a person. A man chooses celibacy thinking he does so for the love of God whereas in fact he has a deep-seated fear of intimacy. Psychological motivations, even unconscious ones, would belong, in Rahner's theory, to the realm of the objective, not to the transcendental openness to God. The psychological can distort the transcendental just as easily as a moral choice.

Finally, we might mention that at least in Rahner's essay on Ignatian discernment, he does not focus on the Christological dimension of discernment.[4] In fact, the basis of his whole theory, rests on his understanding of grace. So on this point we meet a central difficulty in Rahner's theology. How does he link grace to Christ? In fact, he does so, insisting that grace is always ordered to the Christ event. God has always

---

[4] See Avery Dulles, "Finding God's Will: Rahner's Interpretation of the Ignatian Election," in Woodstock Letters 94 (1965), pp. 130-152.

been the God of grace in view of giving us his Son. But some commentators believe that in Rahner's theology Christ appears to be merely the confirmation of the experience of grace rather than the foundation of it[5]. In any event, for discernment, the experience of Christ is fundamental. His life and his values are the ultimate criterion of the God experience. And so, a person making a significant choice, will always want to compare his choice with Christ's life and values. What would Christ do in my place? And indeed this is exactly what St. Ignatius suggests in the Spiritual Exercises, by placing the election in the second week, where the retreatant meditates day and night on the life of Christ.

For Further Reading:

Karl Rahner, "The Logic of Concrete Individual Knowledge," in The Dynamic Element in the Church, Freiburg, 1964, pp. 84-170.

Avery Dulles, "Finding God's Will: Rahner's Interpretation of the Ignatian Election," Woodstock Letters 94 (1965), pp. 130-152.

William A. Barry, "How Do I Know It's God?", America, May 20, 2002, pp. 12-15.

[5] The critique of Hans Urs von Balthasar moves in this direction. See also the study of Patrick Burke, where he highlights the tension between the universal experience of grace and the Christological. Reinterpreting Karl Rahner: A Critical Study of His Major Themes (Fordham University Press, 2002).

CHAPTER FIVE

Jesus the Sacrament of God

Let me state at the outset the goal of Rahner's Christology. He is looking for a way to express our faith in Jesus that does full justice to his humanity. He fears that many people have a mythological idea of Jesus. They see only his divinity. For such people Jesus is God dressed up as a man. Rahner wants to be able to understand Jesus as the humanity of God. In his humanity we see who God is. As Jesus puts it in John 14:9, he who sees me sees the Father.

A key idea here is that Jesus is the self-expression of God. When God expresses himself outwardly (that is, outside his own Trinitarian life) what comes to be is Jesus of Nazareth.

Here Rahner distinguishes between the greater and the lesser self-expression of God. The minor self-expression is the creation. God's creation reflects his being but is not identical with it. In the book of Genesis the man Adam was said to be created in the image and likeness of God. The author of Genesis wanted to say that by the very fact of creation, the creature has a relationship to God. God is the creature's origin and goal.

But there is a greater self-expression, that which comes to pass in the Incarnation. Here God and God's self-expression are perfectly one. In biblical terms we can remember the words of the prologue of St. John's gospel: "The Word became flesh and dwelt amongst us." (Jn. 1:14) In the history of theology, the Church meditated upon this text during the centuries and eventually formulated the doctrine of the Incarnation in precise terms. Jesus Christ is the one eternal divine person of the Logos. But through the Incarnation this divine person exists in two natures, divine and human. These two natures are distinct but they always act together in harmony. The Church's formulation here is very precise. The Church never doubted the full humanity of Jesus. But in the Church's piety, the accent often fell on the one divine person to the neglect of the humanity. Some Church Fathers, for example, when treating of human weaknesses of Jesus such as hunger or thirst, or his human ignorance, suggested that Jesus was merely pretending. Although this type of theology was never endorsed by the Church, many people were affected by it. Often it seemed as though his humanity was swallowed up by his divinity. Rahner wanted to counteract this tendency.

Before explaining Rahner's position in more detail, I would like to make one point about God's self-expression which I think is extremely interesting. According to Rahner the greater self-expression is the condition of possibility for the lesser. In other words the Incarnation is the condition of possibility for the creation. This point is not always easy to grasp. It would seem that first there needs to be a creation if God is going to express himself in it. This is true in a temporal sense. But Rahner wants to make a deeper point, namely that it is God's very ability to express himself perfectly, that allows him to express himself in the creation at all. The greater always grounds the lesser. But in affirming this, Rahner is not wanting merely to make a subtle metaphysical point. He wants to indicate a deep truth of our faith, namely the unity of God's salvific activity. We shouldn't think of the Incarnation as an after-thought. No, God created the world from the beginning with the intention of expressing himself perfectly in it. In other words the goal of the creation is nothing other than the Incarnation. So Rahner links together in a intimate way the doctrine of the creation and the doctrine of the Incarnation. The first Adam existed for the sake of the second Adam. Rahner's position also has another implication. The Incarnation is not just a repair job for sin. In Rahner's perspective God would have become flesh even if humankind hadn't sinned. In this he follows the medieval tradition of Duns Scotus rather than that of Thomas Aquinas.

Returning now to the question of the Incarnation, Rahner developed a theory to understand the reality of Jesus Christ as the sacrament of God in the world. In Rahner's precise German he called Jesus the 'Realsymbol' of God. This is a technical expression and it is one which is practically impossible to render in good English. Rahner distinguishes a real symbol from a sign. When we have a sign such as a traffic light, there is a unity between sign and signified, but this unity is loose and accidental. The green traffic light indicates go, but the color green is chosen arbitrarily. But there are other types of signs, which Rahner calls real symbols, in which there is an intrinsic unity between sign and signified. An example would be a kiss which indicates the love between two persons. When Judas kisses Jesus to betray him, we are repelled because Judas has perverted the nature of this sign. Rahner argues that the best example in our experience of a real symbol is that of our bodies as expressions of ourselves. I have no way to express myself except through my body, body here being understood in a wide sense. Through my language, through my gestures, through writing, through art, I express myself. My body is my insertion in the world. Others have access to me through my body. At the same time I am more than my body. Paradoxically I both have my body and I am my body. So my body is part of me and yet I transcend my body. In short, the I expresses itself through the body. The body is the real symbol of the I.

Rahner takes this theory and applies it to the Trinity and to the Incarnation. In the Trinity the Father expresses himself in his Word. There is a perfect equality and unity between the Father and his Eternal Word. Now when God wishes to express himself outside the Trinity, the Logos expresses himself in the humanity of Jesus. The humanity and the divinity are distinct and yet they are one because the humanity of Jesus belongs intrinsically to the Logos. How this can happen is a mystery. But we can say this much. The Logos creates the humanity as its own and unites this humanity to itself in one and the same act. The humanity of Jesus is created. As created it has its own autonomy. Jesus is really fully human. But this humanity, as created, from the first moment of its existence always belonged to the Logos as its own humanity, that is, as its own self-expression in the world. God manifests himself in history through the human Jesus Christ. If we want to be able to see God, we have to look to Jesus. By seeing him in his humanity, we see the eternal Logos in history.

In Rahner's technical language, Jesus Christ is the real symbol of God. But, as we have seen, symbol for Rahner has a precise meaning, a meaning which is often not grasped in the English word symbol. Therefore, I suggest we use the word sacrament, a word which I believe renders the idea of what Rahner wants to say, but does so in a way which works better in English. Jesus is the sacrament of God in history, that is, that concrete visible earthly reality which perfectly reflects God, because this human sign is God's own reality in the flesh. The sign perfectly reveals the signified. Jesus perfectly reveals God to humankind.

Having tried to express Rahner's ideas in simple language, let me now dare to let Rahner express himself in his own words, "If a theology of symbolic realities is to be written, Christology, the doctrine of the Incarnation, will obviously form the central chapter. And this chapter need almost be no more than an exegesis of the saying: He who sees me sees the Father (Jn. 14:9) There is no need to dwell here on the fact that the Logos is image, likeness, reflection, representation and presence—filled with all the fullness of the Godhead. But if this is true, we can understand the statement: the incarnate Word is the absolute symbol of God in the world, filled as nothing else can be with what is symbolized. He is not merely the presence and revelation of what God is in himself. He is also the expressive presence of what—

or rather, who—God wished to be, in free grace to the world, in such a way, that this divine attitude, once so expressed, can never be reversed but is and remains final and unsurpassable."[1]

Even with explanation, Rahner's language remains dense. But in fact Rahner is saying the same thing as the Church expresses in her Christmas liturgy. In the preface of the Christmas Mass, the Church proclaims: "In the wonder of the Incarnation, Your eternal Word has brought to the eyes of faith a new and radiant vision of your glory. In him we see our God made visible and so are caught up in the love of the God we cannot see." This then is the meaning of the Incarnation: by contemplating the reality of Jesus in the flesh, we are drawn to know the unfathomable depths of God, whom Rahner calls God the Holy Mystery as such. And what is more, this way of knowing God is not only valid for us on earth during the process of our earthly pilgrimage. Rather this way is the way which we must walk for all eternity, for even in the beatific vision, it will always be the case that we will know the Infinite God through the humanity of Jesus. Jesus will always be our way to the Father.[2]

---

[1] Rahner, "On the Theology of the Incarnation," <u>Theological Investigations</u> 4 (London: Darton, Longman and Todd, 1966), p. 237.

[2] See Rahner, "The Eternal Significance of the Humanity of Jesus for our Relationship to God," <u>Theological Investigations</u> 3 (London: Darton, Longman and Todd, 1967), pp. 35-46.

For Further Reading:

Karl Rahner, "On the Theology of the Incarnation," Theological Investigations 4, London, 1974, pp. 105-120.

Karl Rahner, "The Eternal Significance of the Humanity of Jesus for our Relationship with God," Theological Investigations 3, 1974, pp. 35-46.

CHAPTER SIX

The Mystery of Christ's Death

Rahner has always wanted to link together Christian faith in God with an understanding of the human. So consistently, he wants to reflect on the mystery of Christ's death by seeing it in the light of the phenomenon of human death.

Rahner has been in part influenced by the existentialist philosophy of Heidegger. In Heidegger's masterpiece, <u>Being and Time</u>, a large section was devoted to the phenomenon of death. This phenomenon was so important for Heidegger that he dared to call the human person 'being for death'. Heidegger is interested in death as human phenomenon, not primarily as a biological one. As a human phenomenon, we human beings are always in the process of dying. As soon as a man is born, he is old enough to die. Death is the horizon within which we live. On some level we are always reckoning with the possibility of our death even if we do so by some form of avoidance or repression. Heidegger would say that death is the ultimate future for each one of us.

In this context Heidegger, and Rahner following him, speak of death as an event of freedom. Of course I cannot choose not to die. But I can choose how I will die and how I will fashion my life in the face of death. In fact, it is the necessity of choice in the face

47

of death that gives life its seriousness. If life were extended infinitely, it wouldn't matter so much what I do with my life. But I know I only have a limited time in which to live and to accomplish something for myself. So death presses me to take my freedom seriously. Even when biological death approaches, for example, in serious illness, I am confronted with my freedom. I can face death with resignation or rage. I can also face death with serenity and peace, and with concern for others, for example those loved ones I leave behind. I never cease to be human even in the face of death. We see this especially in the face of martyrs but also we have many such testimonies of freedom before death, for example in the concentration camps. The constant threat of death led Victor Frankl to a search for meaningfulness, which later gave birth to his psychological method of logotherapy. In any case, human death implies freedom.

But this is not all. There is another sense in which I experience death as fate. It is something inescapable, moreover something over which I have no control. Before death I am ultimately passive and powerless. Death overcomes me. Death is my fate.

All that I have said thus far can be gleaned more or less from a philosophical reflection upon death. As a human phenomenon death represents both supreme freedom and supreme fate, both liberty and powerlessness.

As a Christian however we need, according to Rahner, to bring in a further reflection. First of all, death as we know it is the death of sin. By this Rahner first of all means that death came into the world by the sin of Adam. In this sense, death was not originally willed by God. Death is something which should not be. Rahner suggests that we can verify this truth existentially in the dread we experience in the face of death. All of us to some extent experience great anguish before death, at the reality of our extinction, at the fact that all our projects are doomed to futility by death. Not even love can survive death, it would seem. The precious faithful love of a husband for his wife or a mother for her child cannot grant immortality to the beloved. Moreover, in all death, there is the shadow of the greatest fear of all, being cut off from what can ultimately fulfil me, being exposed to absolute nothingness, in short the loss of God. The death of sin means the threat of abandonment by God.

Turning now to Christ, the most important thing that Rahner wants to say is that Christ fully embraced our human life and thus also our human death. He experienced life to the full, including death. Moreover, the New Testament affirms that, although Christ was sinless, he died the death of a sinner. He too experienced anguish in the face of death, as we see in the garden of Gethsemane. And on the cross he cried out, "My God, my God why hast Thou forsaken me?" (Mk. 15:34) As regards Christian death, Rahner's principal affirmation is that, because of Christ's death, death can now be for us a death of grace, that is, we can join our death to Christ's as a saving death. Of course, there is also the possibility to refuse to do so. We can reject Christ's death, in which case our death becomes exclusively a death of sin, without hope. The death of sin is the death of despair.

What we have just affirmed makes sense in terms

of the theology of the Incarnation. But how now does Rahner treat the traditional idea of Christ's sacrifice? Here we should note that there are both historical and theological dimensions to our question.

First, Rahner confronts the historical question of how Jesus approached his death. Is there good historical evidence that Jesus thought of his impending death as an expiatory sacrifice? Rahner notes that the scriptural scholars are divided on this question. Certainly there are texts in the New Testament that see the death of Jesus as a sacrifice. One thinks of the institution of the Eucharist and Christ's words that the cup is the cup of the new covenant in his blood (Mk. 14:24). Then there are the texts in which Jesus presents himself as the suffering servant. For example, the famous text in Mark 10:45, "The Son of Man came not to be served, but to serve and give his life as a ransom for many." While we see here that the New Testament interprets Jesus's death as sacrificial, it is not clear whether these texts go back to Jesus himself during his ministry or are they post-resurrection reflections of the first Christian community?

In any case, Rahner believes that it is not essential that Jesus during his ministry understood his death as sacrificial. What is essential is first of all that Jesus saw himself as God's final representative to humankind, that Jesus made an extraordinary claim about his knowledge of the Father and about his authority to fulfil the Father's plan of salvation. It is further necessary that Jesus remained faithful to this mission in the face of the rejection of Israel and in the face of the death, which he surely saw approaching. It is essential that Jesus continued to hope in his Abba God and expected vindication in spite of his death. All these presuppositions, Rahner believes, have good historical and scriptural warrants.

So, for Rahner, the death of Jesus is saving in that Jesus embraced this death willingly and continued to trust in God to the end. And indeed God did vindicate him by raising him from the dead. So God confirmed his mission. Jesus was and is his final offer of salvation. Death did not have power over him, and death did not destroy the mission. Jesus lives and so continues to be God's offer of mercy to humankind.

We might note here that Rahner is obviously intimately linking together the death of Jesus and his resurrection. If Jesus had not been raised, he would not be our Savior. But in fact he has been raised and vindicated. God has made him, as the scriptures say, Lord and Christ. So the first thing that we note is that his death is saving, because of its link to resurrection. It is in the light of his being raised that we can say that his death is salvific.

So can we call it a sacrifice? Yes indeed, but we need to make a number of careful distinctions. First, in the history of religions, sacrifice is generally viewed as a human attempt to reach communion with God. In Christ's case, however, the action proceeds from God to humanity. Jesus is first of all <u>sent</u>. Jesus responds to his mission even unto death. But the primacy of the action belongs with the Father. Secondly, in contrast with the Old Testament or pagan religions Jesus does not offer a thing (animals, wheat etc.) but himself. His sacrifice is his obedience, the gift of himself to the Father and to his brothers and sisters. Thirdly, there is no question of changing

God's mind or overcoming an angry God. This last notion entered into Christian theology especially with Anselm of Canterbury and became very important with certain reformation theologians especially John Calvin. He asserted that God's wrath fell upon Jesus, who bore it voluntarily, so that we could be saved from it. But such a conception has no genuine scriptural basis and Rahner firmly rejects it.

We have said that Rahner accepts Christ's death as sacrificial. We can go on to say that Christ's death causes our salvation. But in what sense? Here Rahner offers, I believe, a very original approach. The death on the cross is not causal by changing something in God. God doesn't have a new attitude to us because of Christ's death. His attitude has always been that of loving kindness and compassion. But the death of Christ has caused a new situation for humankind. Rahner puts it this way. By sending the savior, by becoming incarnate, God posits his definitive Word in history. From the moment of the Incarnation the Word existed in the flesh, with a human history. But by accepting life in its fullness including death, God took death into his own life and overcame it.

Throughout human history God had sought a covenant partner, God had sought a definitive yes from humanity. By Christ's saying yes to the Father throughout life and death, God has found the perfect response. In this sense the issue of human history has been resolved. In this one man Jesus Christ, there is a definitive union between God and humanity, which even sin and death could not break. So human history has found its completion. And Christ lives to draw us into his completion. Through death Christ entered into risen glory and now draws us into a share in that glory.Thus his death and resurrection is the definitive victory of God's grace in the world.This victory can never be threatened. The only thing at stake is whether we choose to participate in Christ's victory by our freedom. History has reached its goal (the God-man). Now we must decide whether we will reach our goal in him.

There is one final point to note here and I think it is of supreme importance. Everything depends on Christ's acceptance of death in his human freedom. In Rahner's mind Christ's surrender to God in free-dom reveals him as a man of faith and hope. For Rahner Christ is not dispensed from faith, rather he is the perfect exemplification of it. But faith here is understood not so much as believing that something is the case, but rather as surrender to God.And Christ, like us, does so in darkness, indeed even in the bitter darkness of the abandonment of the cross. Rahner writes,"According to Scripture we may safely say that Jesus in his life was the <u>believer</u>… and that he was constantly the one who hopes absolutely and in regard to God and men obviously the one who loves absolutely. In the unity of this triplicity of faith, hope and love, Jesus surrendered himself in his death unconditionally to the absolute mystery that he called his Father, into whose hands he committed his existence, when in the night of his death and God-for-saken-ness he was deprived of everything that is oth-erwise regarded as the content of a human existence: life, honor, acceptance in earthly and relgious fellow-ship and so on. In the concreteness of his death it becomes only too clear that everything fell away from him, even the perceptible security of the closeness of God's love, and in this trackless dark there prevailed silently only the mystery that in itself and in its freedom has no name and to which he nevertheless calmly surrendered himself as to eternal love and not to the hell of futility."[1]

Having looked at how Rahner develops his theology of the saving death of Christ, we can now ask how that death can become a saving reality for us. How do we live the mystery of our death in faith? How can our death become a death 'in the Spirit', a death of grace? For Rahner the center of Christian faith remains the cross of Christ. Everything depends on whether his cross was ultimate, ignominious defeat or the triumphant self-gift of love leading to resurrection. The Christian believes the latter. So Christian faith is fundamentally risking all on the cross of Christ. My surrender to the Mystery of God in faith is linked to my risking all on the cross of Christ. For it is here in human history that the Mystery of God is revealed fully as self-giving love. Every man and woman experiences in life a measure of darkness, suffering, sickness, failure, and isolation and all these are foreshadowings of death. So each of us is challenged: in the face of these darknesses do I despair or do I turn to Christ and his cross and risk my all on his death? Again Rahner insists: either his death is the triumph of God's project in history or humankind is condemned to a longing which will never be filled.

---

[1] Rahner, "Following the Crucified," Theological Investigations 13 (London: Darton, Longman, Todd, 1975), p. 165.

For Rahner, believing in Christ means following the Crucified One. Christ went to glory through the abandonment of Calvary. The road to the Kingdom was through the narrow door. And so it must be for us. This means that there is no path to God except through sharing in the cross. In some way then we have to share his darkness. Life will offer such darknesses inevitably in our sicknesses, failures, loneliness. In these moments God invites me to associate these sufferings with those of Christ. But there is something more. Christians can voluntarily deny themselves some human created goods in order to participate in Christ's cross. Many renunciations will be given by life. Others can be chosen to prepare us for the renunciation which each of us must inevitably make, that of earthly life itself in death. We do this because we know in faith that Christ walked this path and his cross, which seemed ultimate defeat, was in fact the entrance to the fullness of life. So renunciation is part of Christian life, but not in a negative, life-denying way, but with a realism that loves life but which also recognizes that there is a fuller life which transcends life as we know it here and now.

Rahner says that embracing Christ's cross offers us a life without illusions. Our contemporary technological culture tries to persuade us that we can fix everything. All our sufferings can be overcome. Ours is a youth culture and now we even have cosmetic surgery to remove the wrinkles and tuck in the extra fat. We have sexual liberation and so sensual pleasure is easy to come by without apparent responsibility. But deeper reflection reveals that we inevitably grow old, decline and die. Sensual pleasures, bought cheaply, backfire with unwanted pregnancy and sexually transmitted diseases. Ironically, those proficient in information technology, are finding employment hard to come by in an over-glutted market. In short, death in all its forms and in all its shadows remains life's ultimate riddle. The Christian, Rahner affirms, can look death in the face, participate in it, but not be overwhelmed by it, for his hope is in Christ dead and risen.

Finally, the Christian is committed to love as Christ loves. His life is based on Christ's, "who loved his own to the end." (Jn. 13:1) This is not romantic love nor is it love based on mutual self-interest. It is a love which has the power to give even when there is no apparent reward. In loving, one takes up one's cross. At first loving might seem attractive. Secular humanistic love might seem a romantic ideal. But, as Rahner says, this illusion must be 'undeceived'.[2] I must learn how to love when it begins to hurt, when there is lack of reciprocity, or even when the other betrays me. And I must do this not in a heroic way, but simply because that is what is means to be a follower of Christ. The ultimate stage of discipleship is to continue to love, even when one sees that love does not or no longer pays off.

The conclusion of Rahner's theological reflection is that the cross is at the center of the three great virtues of faith, hope and love: of faith, because believing in God for a Christian means embracing

---

[2] On the cross as life without illusions and love 'undeceived', see Rahner, "Self-Realisation and Taking Up One's Cross," Theological Investigations 13, p. 256.

Christ's cross as the sign of God's victory in history; of hope, because the cross carries with it the promise of life beyond the grave; and of charity, for taking up one's cross is ultimately nothing other than love of one's neighbor, accepting Christ's example of the foot-washing, living his new commandment, to love even as he first loved us.

For Further Reading:

Karl Rahner, <u>On The Theology of Death</u>, Freiburg, 1961.

Karl Rahner, <u>Foundations of Christian Faith</u>, London, 1978, pp. 254-255, 282-285.

Karl Rahner, "Following the Crucified," <u>Theological Investigations</u> 18, London, 1984 , pp. 157-170.

CHAPTER SEVEN

The Sacred Heart

Rahner wrote numerous articles on the Sacred Heart. This is not surprising since the Sacred Heart devotion has been a key aspect of Jesuit spirituality throughout the centuries. In fact, the symbol Christology, which we looked at in chapter four, was first developed by Rahner to understand devotion to the heart of Jesus. Let us look at this devotion in its theological dimensions.

Devotion to the heart of Christ in one sense is as old as the New Testament. In John 19:34, we are told how Christ's heart was pierced with a lance and blood and water flowed out. The pierced side of Christ reveals the depths of Christ's love for us, to the point that it is emptied out in compassion for men and women. However more particularly, the devotion, as we know it today, emerged in 17th century France. Its key proponent was St. Margaret Mary Alacoque (1647-1690). Her confessor was the Jesuit Father, canonized recently by John Paul II in 1992, Claude de la Colombière. Through him the devotion was adopted by the Jesuits and quickly grew to become a wide-spread devotion among Catholics. Two aspects of it are particularly noteworthy. First, this devotion appeared in France at the time of the Jansensist spirituality. This spirituality was noted for its moral and ascetical rigorism. Certainly Jansensism encouraged Christians to take their faith and its demands seriously, but to say the least, it produced a gloomy and Pelagian-oriented Christianity[1]. Devotion to the heart of Christ, by contrast, stressed the mercy of Christ, symbolized by his open heart.

The second important aspect was the idea of reparation. In the 17th century there was a great awareness of indifference toward religion. Especially among the more wealthy classes, life was given often to the pursuit of pleasure. Religious practice was neglected. There was often a practical atheism. Margaret Mary, for example, recorded these words of Christ to her: "Behold this Heart which has so loved human beings that it has spared nothing, even to exhausting and consuming itself, in order to give them proof of its love, and in return I receive from the greater number nothing but ingratitude, contempt, irreverence, sacrilege and coldness in this sacrament of my love." The Sacred Heart devotion called men and women to repair the terrible sins and sacrileges committed against the heart of Jesus. Jesus died for sinners and yet the heart of human beings had grown cold with indifference. The preaching of the Sacred Heart was a call to conversion.

The Sacred Heart devotion raised a number of theological questions. One was whether it was legitimate to adore the human heart of Christ. It might seem odd to worship a particular part of the body of

---

[1] Pelagius was an Irish monk of the fifth century who taught that human beings can win salvation through their own efforts. He was fiercely opposed by St. Augustine.

Christ. Pope Pius XII taught that the heart of Christ was worthy of worship because it is inseparably united to the Divine Word.[2] An implication of this approach would be that one could worship any part of Christ such as his feet or lips.[3]

Rahner developed an original approach to the theology of the Heart of Christ. First of all, he saw the 'heart' not as the physical heart of Christ's human body. Rather for him the heart represented one of those original symbolic words in human speech. Such words are opposed to technical words which are functional. These symbolic words have an immense evocative power, they have an enormous power of persuasion, and are capable of arousing multiple feelings and associations. So for Rahner the heart is a primordial word. This word indicates the center of the person. In fact, Rahner would say that only a human being has a heart. So the word 'heart' indicates the whole of the human being in his spiritual and bodily reality. From this center there streams forth who the person is. What is central and interior, the heart of the person, manifests itself in the exterior world. The heart of the human being becomes visible in his words and actions. The heart, in fact, indicates the core of his existence. Rahner also notes that the heart as such does not indicate love. The center of the person can be filled with love, or equally with indifference or hate.

In this context Rahner explains devotion to the heart of Christ. The corporeal heart of Christ is really

[2] Encyclical Letter, Haurietis Aquas, 1956.
[3] This approach may be technically correct theologically, but isn't particularly helpful on the devotional level.

a symbol of the center of Christ's being. When we honor the heart of Christ, we are honoring the center of his person. In the case of Christ, his center is that of the divine love. Christ is the revelation of the Father's love and mercy, a love which reaches out to all, especially those who are sinners, and especially those in situations of crisis, the abandoned, the outcast, those in danger of death. So, the heart of Christ is a powerful symbol for those who feel abandoned and it is specially powerful for us human beings when we are faced with the imminence of our death, that moment when we are confronted with our impotence in an inescapable way.

Let us now come to the question of reparation. This is a very tricky theme in theology and one which can land us in serious trouble if misunderstood. As I said, reparation was a key aspect of the traditional devotion. And part of the devotion was the holy hour, in which the believer remained before the Blessed Sacrament exposed, to make reparation to Christ for the sins committed against his heart. Sometimes, this was interpreted as if the prayer before the Blessed Sacrament alleviated the physical sufferings of Christ during his passion. A number of points here need to be clarified. First, it is important to remember that Christ in the Blessed Sacrament is the glorified Christ. Christ in his glory suffers no more. Secondly, one would have to ask whether our present prayers now can take away the suffering of Christ thousands of years ago. Perhaps one could say that since God is eternal, he applied our present prayers to relieve the suffering of Christ long ago. Still it is questionable whether this is the best approach to the meaning of reparation.

Let me suggest another approach as Rahner develops it in his writings. First, we need to bring in the concept of the Mystical Body. Christ is united to his people here and now. The Glorified Christ has not abandoned us but is still with us. So, in that sense, the sufferings of the world continue to affect Christ. As St. Paul says Col. 1:24, "In my flesh I complete what is lacking in Christ's afflictions for the sake of his body, that is, the church." Secondly, if we love Christ, then we want to share in his mission and his mission was and is to reach out to sinners, to heal, to show compassion, and to overcome the power of evil. So repairing means overcoming the effects of sin in the world. It means co-operating with the present work of Christ, continuing to share in his mission. Christ vanquished sin on the cross. We must continue to labor with him to vanquish sin and its effects in the world today. For sin continues to impede his reign and Christ invites us to collaborate with him in bringing about his Kingdom. This, of course, not in a Pelagian way. Rather we collaborate with Christ, giving his grace the priority.

We mentioned above that the rise of the devotion in the 17th century stressed the godlessness of the world. The devotion has always stressed the shining forth of God's love and mercy from the heart of Christ in a darkened world. But precisely these aspects continue to be relevant today. In our world as well, there is a great deal of practical atheism. Moreover, our world is particularly violent. We live in an age of mass terrorism in which ordinary people feel under threat every day. We live in a world where there is a trafficking of children for sexual pleasure.

We live in a world where we see abuse of children and adolescents in the churches and even in the family. So it is appropriate to preach the victory of Christ's love in the midst of our own contemporary darknesses.

In this context reparation means two things. First it means laboring with Christ to eliminate these evils and secondly it means the prayer of intercession to God. And this intercession can be made most fittingly to the heart of Christ. No prayer remains without its efficacy. All of us are bound together in solidarity. The beauty of the Mystical Body is that the solidarity of one part necessarily is efficacious for another part, even if that efficacy is hidden from our eyes and even if we do not know on this earth who has benefited by our prayer. So we express our love and gratitude to the heart of Christ by working to eradicate evil from this world and by praying to him especially for those sinners most engulfed by the darkness of sin and most in need of his mercy. In this sense devotion to the heart of Christ is as relevant as it has ever been.[4]

For Further Reading:

Karl Rahner, "'Behold the Heart!' Preliminaries to a Theology of the Sacred Heart, <u>Theological Investigations</u> 3, London, 1974, pp. 321-330.

Karl Rahner, "Some Theses For a Theology of Devotion to the Sacred Heart," <u>Theological Investigations</u> 3, pp. 331-352.

[4] For another effort to use Rahner to explain the importance of the Sacred Heart devotion today, see Philip Endean, "Karl Rahner and the heart of Christ," <u>The Month</u> (1977), pp. 357-363.

Karl Rahner, "The Theological Meaning of the Veneration of the Sacred Heart," <u>Theological Investigations</u> 8, 1971, pp. 217-228.

Philip Endean, "Karl Rahner and the Heart of Christ," <u>The Month</u>, 1997, pp. 357-363.

CHAPTER EIGHT

The Church As Mystery

Catholic theology stresses that the Church is Mystery. In the context of Rahner's theology such an assertion makes eminent sense. The heart of theology is the Mystery of God and God becomes visible through Christ and his Church. If the Church is a Mystery (like God), then the Church cannot be reduced to an object. No sociological analysis will ever do full justice to the Church. Such an approach is very difficult in our age and for many people is unintelligible, since Mystery is quite eclipsed in our functional culture.

If the Church is Mystery, it follows that a correct understanding of the Church is only possible in faith. The Church is a Mystery of faith. It is no accident that in the Creed, the believer's profession of faith in the Church comes under the third article, belief in the Holy Spirit. Only the Holy Spirit or grace makes faith in the Church possible.

Rahner stresses that God saves us first as a people. Christ chooses a people as his own. Christ unites himself with his Bride. Christ the Head unites himself with his Mystical Body. The point is that an individual person must insert himself into this reality. In a certain sense the Church anticipates the faith of any member. The Church has its origin in Christ's choice.

Hence it is not like any other organization where the members first decide to constitute the group.

This puts the individual believer in a paradoxical situation. He or she believes what the Church believes. Concretely the believer learns this in the catechumenate, by entering into the mystagogy of Christ. So that means that the individual does not stand outside or above the Church sitting in judgment on the Church. Rather, the individual believer is constantly struggling to make his faith adequate to that of the Church, to what the Church believes.[1]

As I say, this is a paradox. For at the same time the Church is not dispensed from thinking, nor from the struggle to understand her faith. The Church has struggled for centuries to grasp the central truths of her existence, such as the Trinity and the Incarnation. But the individual believer submits himself to the faith of the community which is bigger than he is and which has the assistance of the Holy Spirit. Even the Holy Scripture cannot place itself above the Church, as though the Scriptures decide the truth of the Church. Of course the Church lives under the Word of God. But at the same time this is in no way a slavery, for the Church herself has produced the Scriptures as her own book.

What I am trying to say in all this is that the Church is a mystery of faith, a mystery which can be grasped only in faith. Any other approach is doomed to failure from the start.

[1] On the believer's act of faith in the Church, see K. Rahner, "I believe in the Church," Theological Investigations 7 (London: Darton, Longman and Todd, 1971), pp. 100-118.

The Church as Sacrament of God's Grace

We have seen that the key to Rahner's spirituality is that every human person has the opportunity for a direct experience of God. At the same time because we human beings always live in history, our experience of God must become tangible and visible in space and time. In fact for Rahner God's offer of grace always leads us in principle toward the Christ-event which represents the fulfilment of God's purposes for the world and the triumph of God's grace in history.

At the same time, for Christian faith, Christ has not just disappeared from history after his death and resurrection. He continues to abide with us in his Spirit and his Spirit becomes visible in the Church.

There are many images used to express the reality of the Church and none of them fully captures the mystery of the Church. The Second Vatican Council highlighted the nature of the Church as the People of God. But significantly the Council also chose to refer to the Church as a sacrament. In the first number of the Council's Constitution on the Church, we read, "By her relationship with Christ the Church is a kind of sacrament of intimate union with God, and of the unity of all mankind, that is, she is a sign and an instrument of such union and unity." Later in no. 48, Lumen Gentium repeats the same idea: "Rising from the dead, Christ sent his life-giving Spirit upon his disciples and through his Spirit has established his body, the Church, as the universal sacrament of salvation."

This guiding idea of the Council becomes Rahner's principal way of thinking about the Church. We have already seen in Rahner's study of Christ that Jesus can be seen as the sacrament of God. In Jesus God becomes visible. In the humanity of Jesus we see who God is. Jesus said as much in John 14:9, "He who sees me sees the Father."

Something similar can be said about the Church. Through the Church Christ continues to live in history. The Church renders Christ visible. In fact, the Council spoke of the union between Christ and the Church as similar to the union between Christ's divine Person and his human nature. But we have to be careful here. Since Christ is the divine Person, his humanity perfectly expresses the divinity. But the Church is not divine. The Church is made up of human beings who are sinners. So the Church never perfectly reflects the divinity. For this reason the Council spoke of an analogy between the Incarnation and the Church.

Still the Church does express Christ. In the Scriptures, in the sacraments, in the teaching office, in the holiness of Christians, Christ remains visibly present in history. And because of Christ's victory over sin and death and because of the outpouring of the Holy Spirit upon the Church, the Church will never fail to reflect the glory of her Lord. God's grace will always shine forth in her.

Viewing the Church as the sacrament of Christ is important for it constantly reminds us of the mission of the Church. Vatican II spoke of Christ as Lumen Gentium, Light to the nations (no. 1). Because the Church shares in this light, she has the mission to be the light of God in this world. If we Christians see ourselves as called to be the sacrament of God's presence, we will seek all the more to be light and to let our light radiate in history.

At this point, it would be worthwhile to say a brief word about the Church as sacrament and the seven sacraments. The Council of Trent defined that there are seven sacraments and that Christ instituted them. How we understand this today is not immediately evident. We have more historical consciousness today than did the Council Fathers at Trent. It is not clear from the Scriptures when Christ established certain sacraments, for example, marriage. But Rahner thinks we can find a solution, by seeing the seven sacraments as embodiments of the one primordial sacrament of the Church. With his resurrection Christ established his Church. And the seven sacraments are realizations of the Church, privileged moments when the Church acts on behalf of her members, in critical moments of their lives. In these moments we have the guarantee of Christ's presence and assisting grace because of the efficacy of the sacraments.

Here we touch upon the interesting question of the grace of the sacraments. The sacraments are efficacious because of Christ's grace. Christ guarantees his presence and offer of grace. But how should we conceive this? Rahner goes back to the classical idea that the sacraments cause grace by signifying. That is, they cause grace by being the signs which they are. In earlier chapters we have studied Rahner's idea of grace and shown how grace is universally present in our world. God is constantly offering his grace to everyone. Hence the sacraments don't cause grace for the first time. Grace is already present. But the sacraments do signify grace, that is, they make grace visible, and by making it visible they intensify and increase the grace already present.

Perhaps a few examples would help. A husband loves his wife. But he doesn't want his love to remain merely interior. He wants to express it. So he kisses her. The kiss doesn't create the love, but it expresses it and in so doing the love becomes deeper and is increased. In the same way, an adult before baptism receives grace. God is present in his life as he gets to know Christ and undergoes a conversion experience. As he joins the catechumenate the love is becoming visible. In the sacrament of baptism the grace reaches its full efficacy in the sacramental sign, as he is incorporated into the Church. Or again, a man who has turned away from God, begins to undergo a conversion experience. Under God's grace he feels sorrow and repents of his sin. Thus God's grace is already at work in him, but when he goes to the sacrament of reconciliation, this grace is deepened through the positing of the sign. His grace becomes visible in the sacramental action. The sacrament thus expresses and deepens God's grace within him.

The Church Holy But Sinful

In confessing the Apostles' Creed, we say 'I believe in the holy Catholic Church'. Yet as Catholics we confess our sins at the beginning of every Eucharist, and indeed we have a sacrament specifically to receive God's pardon for our sins. Isn't this a contradiction, that we say both that the Church is holy and yet acknowledge that those belonging to the Church are sinners? Indeed is it legitimate to speak of the

Church itself as sinful? In the reflections that follow I hope to show that we are not dealing with a contradiction but with a paradox that leads us to the center of the Church's Mystery.

Often today one sees two radically different tendencies in thinking about the Church. One is quite idealistic and stresses the transcendence of the Church and her mission in history. The supernatural character of the Church is stressed. In this vision the Eucharist, for example, represents on earth the heavenly banquet. The Pope is seen as Christ's vicar on earth and so on.

The other side is to emphasize the Church's defects and the terrible sins of her members. In the United States we are painfully aware of the betrayal of our bishops in not protecting our children and we are deeply pained by the crimes of some of our priests. The press delight in uncovering the corruptions of the Church.

In fact, both these dimensions are stressed in the Scriptures. The Letter to the Ephesians stresses the Church without spot or wrinkle (5:27). But the gospels equally present parables such as the haul of fish (Mt. 13:47-50) or the tares and the wheat (Mt. 13:36-43) which indicate that on this earth Christ's Church will always be a mixture of the good and the bad.

Throughout history there have always been attempts to create the perfect Church. In the third century there were the Montanists who rejected the body and wanted to live as if they were already in the Kingdom. In the Middle Ages Joachim of Fiore thought that a new age was about to dawn, the age of the Spirit, in which the institutional Church would no longer be necessary. The spiritual Franciscans wanted to reject all use of money or material goods. In the seventeenth century the Jansenists proposed a rigorist form of Christian asceticism.

But these movements have always been condemned by the Church as extremist. The Church knows herself to be a church of sinners.

Still how should we conceive of the Church as holy and sinful? Indeed can we say that the Church is sinful or merely that there are sinners in the Church? This is a key problem about which Rahner reflects and seeks to find a solution.

Minimally we must say, according to Rahner, that there are and always will be sinners in the Church. Lumen Gentium, no. 14, explicitly says so[2]. Hence a utopian idealism is to be rejected at once. The approach of the Council is to say that sinners belong to the visible structure of the Church, but they do not belong to her heart. For they reject the grace of God which the Church wishes to make visible. Just as a sinner can receive the sacrament of the Eucharist without receiving grace (for his heart is hardened in his sin), so a sinner can belong to the Church without belonging to the heart of the Church. Effectively he is a dead member, although God's grace will

---

[2] "They are fully incorporated into the society of the church who, possessing the Spirit of Christ, accept its whole structure and all the means of salvation that have been established within it, and within its visible framework are united with Christ, who governs it through the supreme pontiff and bishops, by the bonds of profession of faith, the sacraments, ecclesiastical government and communion. That person is not saved, however, even though he might be incorporated into the church, who does not persevere in charity; he does indeed remain in the bosom of the church 'bodily', but not 'in his heart'."

74

always pursue him seeking a response of love as long as he lives.

At the same time Rahner says that there is a sense in which we can say that the Church itself is sinful. This is because the sins of the Church affect the Church. It is not as though the Church remains impervious to the sins of her members. They affect the body and render the light of Christ more dim. In this sense the Council says that the Church must always seek to purify herself. She must seek a continual conversion as she makes her way through the pilgrimage of history.

How then can we say that the Church is holy? Augustine's answer was that the Church is indefectibly holy in the means of grace which Christ makes available through her: the scriptures, the sacraments, the teachings of the faith. Rahner obviously thinks this is true. But he wishes to say something more. For him, the Church is holy because of the victory of Christ's grace in the cross and resurrection. Christ has triumphed once and for all and his victory will never be lacking in history. We know this because the risen Christ pledges the gift of the Holy Spirit to the Church. In this sense there is a guarantee of the holiness of the Church. Christ promises that holiness will never be lacking. The grace of Christ will never fail completely. God will always raise up holy men and women in the Church in which his grace will shine forth, so that the world can see the holiness of God and witness God's triumphant love for the world. Because of the Holy Spirit, given with the paschal mystery, the Church will always be a sign of grace in spite of the sins of her members.

In the great jubilee of 2000, the Church made a profound admission along these lines when she confessed her sins of the past. Pope John Paul II asked divine forgiveness for the great sins of her sons and daughters in the past such as sins against the Jews. Reflecting upon this, the International Theological Commission in its document <u>Memory and Reconciliation</u> (March 7, 2000) wrote, "The Church knows that she is not only a community of the elect, but one which in her very bosom, includes the righteous and sinners, of the present as well as the past, in the unity of the Mystery which constitutes her." (introduction to chapter 3) But the same commission goes on to stress that the deeper reality is not just the presence of sinners in the bosom of the Church but the fact that their sins wound the church. The Body of Christ is weakened by the sins of Christians. The theologians cite St. Ambrose, "Let us beware lest our fall become a wound of the Church." (3:3) Hence once again an awareness of our sinfulness is a summons to mission. We are summoned to become Lumen Gentium. But our sins dim the light of Christ, and obscure Christ's presence in the world. Hence the summons to become what we truly are by our baptism, the light of God's grace in this world.

Church and World

Rahner's writings on the Church are vast. Since most of his writings were occasional, he often developed themes on which he was asked to lecture. Not only did he think theologically about the Church. He also asked himself concretely how the Church should look and function in the world today. Many of his points remain, I believe, valid for us some twenty years after his death.

Rahner grew up in a Germany where the Churches had much political power and social prestige. In his youth it was still the case that one almost inherited one's religion through family and geography. One per force belonged to the Protestant Church or the Catholic one. One paid a church tax according to one's religion. There was still much prestige in being a clergymen, especially a bishop. Being a Catholic in this situation very often didn't amount to a free choice. It was part of the culture.

Rahner saw this situation change but he also thought the change was positive and that it should continue in the future. On the one hand he took up the stress on the local community which he discovered in Vatican II. In no. 26 of Lumen Gentium, we read, "In any community existing around an altar, under the sacred ministry of the bishop, there is manifested a symbol of that charity and 'unity of the Mystical Body, without which there can be no salvation.' In these communities, though frequently small and poor, or living far from any another, Christ is present." The Council is here thinking of the diocese as local church, but the idea could be extended to parishes, base communities or other groups of Christians such as found in the various movements. What for Rahner is important in all this is the fact that Church life will be based on small groups where a fraternal atmosphere will prevail. The freedom of choice to belong to the church will play a far larger role than in the past. Catholicism will no longer just be cultural but will involve a free commitment.

Another idea which continually recurs in Rahner's writings is that of diaspora. Christendom or a Christian society is a thing of the past. The Church can longer expect that the majority will live according to Christian faith and morality. The Church can no longer expect to impose its way of life upon society. In the post war years, Western Europe was dominated by Christian democratic parties. Rahner sees this era as over.

In such a situation two attitudes are possible. One can lament the lack of influence and turn inward seeking to muster as much influence as possible in the way of a sect, or one can see the situation as an invitation to bear witness. For Rahner the Church of the future will be a little flock. But this doesn't make it a sect. Rather these little communities of the Church will be communities of witness, communities that preach the gospel and that seek to live the gospel beatitudes and hence to be a light to the world. In this sense for Rahner the diaspora situation is positive.

How then should Christians conceive the world? One way would be to see the world as evil, to see culture as basically hostile to the gospel. According to this vision there is an apocalyptic struggle between the Church and its values and the world and its non-values. The other attitude, which is Rahner's, is to see the world as the sphere of God's grace. God is everywhere operative in the world and in history. God is continually summoning men and women to transcend themselves in gift to God and to one another. In this context Rahner sees great possibilities for collaboration between the Church and culture. The Church and its leaders should seek points of agreement, points where collaboration is possible, such as social justice. Secular culture is not seen as a hostile force but as a dialogue partner.

Mission in a New Context

The Church exists for mission. How will men and women today be able to find God? How will they discover God's purposes for the world? They will do this through the Church and through its preaching of the gospel. They will do so as well through the holiness which can be seen in the lives of believers.

Rahner never tires of speaking of God's grace operating in the hearts of all men and women. But he is equally insistent that grace must be historical, tangible and visible. The one unmistakable and unsurpassable moment in which God's grace triumphed in history is the Incarnation and the death and resurrection of Christ. So all grace leads us to the Christ event. And the risen Christ leads us to his Church, where he is bodily present.

In this way Rahner would insist that every man and woman has a relationship to the Church. God is directing all to Christ and hence it is God's project that all find themselves in the Church. Grace has an inner direction. It is a dynamic movement toward Christ and his Church.

However Rahner recognizes a new situation today. In former times, the Church assumed that the vast part of humanity was lost. Only a few would be saved. The Church preached to men and women as though they would come to know God and his mercy for the first time in the Church's missionary activity. Today that presupposition is no longer valid.

Rather the man or woman who hears the gospel has already been touched by God's grace. God's grace has been preparing the soil of the gospel. So in coming to Christ, the believer is really coming to himself. The grace that has been at work in him is taking on visible form. It is becoming tangible in his human history.

I think one cannot emphasize too much the fact that for Rahner what is interior must become exterior. God really wants to take on flesh and blood. He wants to become incarnate. So it is never enough to see a person's relation to God as something interior alone. Yes, grace is present and working. Yes, grace can be responded to in freedom, even in hidden and anonymous ways. But grace never wants to remain inchoate and anonymous. It wants to shine forth and take on clear contours. When grace is effective, it becomes incarnational and ecclesial. Just as parents show their love for their children by clothing them, feeding them and offering them an education, so God's love becomes concrete and tangible in his word, in his sacraments, in his pastors, in the testimony of the saints and martyrs. As St. Ignatius says, love manifests itself in deeds[3] and God's love manifests itself in the community of the Church.

So the Church has the mission to spread the light of Christ everywhere in the world. That is why the Church has the mission to be everywhere, to be a herald to individuals, proclaiming the triumph of God's grace but also to make that grace visible to all nations, peoples and cultures.

[3] "Contemplation to Obtain the Love of God," Spiritual Exercises, no. 230.

For Further Reading:

Karl Rahner, <u>The Church and the Sacraments</u>, Freiburg, 1966.

Karl Rahner, "I Believe in the Church," <u>Theological Investigations</u> 7, London, 1971, pp, 100-118.

Karl Rahner, "The Church of Sinners," <u>Theological Investigations</u> 6, London, 1969, pp. 253-269.

Karl Rahner, "Anonymous Christianity and the Missionary Task of the Church," <u>Theological Investigations</u> 12, London, 1974, pp. 161-178.

CHAPTER NINE

Christian Vocations

Often in theology, when one speaks of the third person of the Blessed Trinity, one speaks of the subjective dimension and the objective dimension of the Holy Spirit. The subjective dimension indicates the holiness which the Holy Spirit creates in the believer, the believer's share in the divine life. The objective dimension indicates how the Holy Spirit becomes institutional in history, for example in the Church's teaching office, ministers and sacraments. One of the ways the Holy Spirit becomes objective is through concrete vocations within the ecclesial community. To use the language of Hans Urs von Balthasar, each vocation has its own form, which gives it a distinct character. In this chapter, I would like to reflect upon Rahner's writings on vocation with particular emphasis on priesthood, marriage, and the religious life.

Let us begin with priesthood. Rahner has a vast number of essays on priesthood. Some of his writings on this topic were presented as part of spiritual conferences or spiritual exercises for priests. Other writings were more strictly theological. Rahner was no doubt inspired by the Second Vatican Council's new vision of priesthood. He tried to reflect on the theological underpinnings of this vision as well as the pastoral implications of it.

In short, priesthood in the Catholic Church from the time of the Middle Ages to the beginning of the Council focused particularly on the cultic dimension of priesthood. The priest was seen as one whose place was at the altar. He had the mission to celebrate the sacraments, especially the Eucharist and penance. He had the power to consecrate the eucharistic elements and to forgive sins.

Vatican II created a new balance by situating the priesthood of the ordained within the priesthood of all the baptized. These two types of priesthood are ordered to one another. The Council also emphasized other dimensions of priesthood, namely the ministry of the Word and the pastoral ministry. Indeed, the Decree on the Ministry and Life of Priests (Prsbyterorum Ordinis) places the ministry of the Word in the first place as regards the duties of the priest. And it identified pastoral charity as the key which would link together all the different aspects of what a priest does in his pastoral work. In the perspective of this decree, the sacramental ministry is situated in the third place. This doesn't mean that it is not important, only that the Council gives a new perspective. The priest is not primarily a man of cult, but rather primarily an apostle whose apostolic work culminates in the celebration of the Eucharist.

Rahner naturally takes as his starting point the priesthood of Christ. In the history of religions there are two dimensions which repeatedly manifest themselves, namely that of sacrifice and that of prophecy. The former is the human being's attempt from below to reach God. The latter is God's free initiative in addressing humanity. Christ combines in himself both dimensions and radically reinterprets them. Christ offers the perfect sacrifice by offering himself. But Christ's sacrifice is not an attempt from the human side to reach God. Rather all the initiative is with the Father. Christ responds to the Father's saving will in obedience. Since Christ is the God-man, his sacrifice is perfect and does not need repetition. It is once for all. Christ's ministry is not only priestly. It is also prophetic. During his life Christ exercised a preaching ministry. He preached the word of the Kingdom. Indeed the Kingdom of God became present in history in his preaching and in the signs he worked. Thus, for example, he preached the mercy of God for sinners and put this into action by eating with tax-collectors and prostitutes. On the cross the Word of God was reduced to silence. Christ entered into Sheol, the realm of the dead, but the Father raised him up. A first consequence of this is the kerygma or preaching of the good news: "The Lord has risen and appeared to Simon." (Lk. 24:34) The resurrection brings about the birth of the Church and the preaching of the gospel.

We have already seen that Christ is the sacrament of God in this world. For Rahner, since God is beyond the world, if he wishes to be present in this world, he must reveal himself and that means a free self-disclosure on his part. Rahner argues that revelation always implies a sign which is freely posited. It cannot be some object in this world like a sacred rock or otherwise it wouldn't be free or indeed supernatural. Revelation posits the sign, and the sign, precisely because it is God's gratuitous action, needs to be interpreted. This is the function of the word. The word indicates the meaning of the sign. So as we just indicated above, Jesus performs many gestures, such as healings, exorcisms, prophetic gestures such as his baptism and his giving of himself in the eucharistic actions of the last supper and he interprets these signs in terms of his presence as the coming of God's Kingdom on earth.

Christian ministry in the Church, and in particular the ordained priesthood, continues Christ's work on earth after his ascension. How should we understand this ministry? Rahner notes that in a certain sense Christian ministry is relativized. Why? Because only Christ fulfils God's ministry in a perfect sense and Christ is never replaced. Thus, for example, the priest does not create the word to be preached. He receives the word. The Church has only one gospel. The ordained priest must preach this gospel adapting it to the needs of a congregation in a given place and time. Likewise with the Eucharist (the cultic aspect). The priest doesn't create the sacrifice. Christ alone offers the sacrifice and it is not repeated. Rather the priest re-presents Christ's sacrifice. The once for all sacrifice of the cross becomes present here and now on the altar through the ministry of the ordained priest.

Still the question remains for Rahner: why is priesthood a sacrament? What distinguishes priesthood from a job, even a noble job like that of a physician or teacher? We know that a sacrament confers grace and this grace is pledged irrevocably. Why does the man who will be a priest need this sacrament?

Rahner responds in terms of his theology of the Word. The Word of God will be credible only if it is preached with conviction, only if it receives testimony from the one who preaches it. In this sense the priest has to preach the Word with his whole being. Preaching can never be a part-time job. If the priests in the Church are to fulfil this demanding vocation they have need of the grace of office, for if this grace were lacking, the situation could result that there would no longer be a credible preaching of the Word of God. In this case the triumph of Christ's life, death and resurrection would be lost in history. The Church would not be able to fulfil her divine vocation. So Rahner argues that the Church is given by Christ the sacrament of orders with its infallible pledge of the grace of office, the grace by which the minister's life can conform to his mission. Obviously this requires as well that the priest freely respond to this grace given to him in the sacrament.

Rahner chooses to work with the ministry of the Word arguing that in this ministry we see the full time character of priesthood. Indeed he also says that cult takes but a small part of the priest's time. So he doesn't want to base his argument for the sacramental character of orders on the cultic dimension. But I think one could make a similar argument for the Eucharist as Rahner makes for preaching the Word. Even if the priest takes but a brief time out of his day to celebrate the Eucharist, the sacrament will not be credible if his life does not conform to the sacrificial action. Hence the classic exhortation during the rite of ordination: imitamini quod tractatis, that is, imitate what you do. So one could argue that Christ gives the priest the sacrament of orders so that he has the grace necessary so that his life conforms to the sacrifice he offers. Indeed the whole school of Sulpician spirituality was oriented in this way. A sacrificial spirituality was proposed that corresponded to the central cultic act of the priest. A circle was created between the sacrificial life of the priest and the sacrifice of the mass he celebrated.

The ministry of the Word also gives the key to priestly spirituality. The priest preaches the Word and indeed does so, practically speaking, every day as he delivers a brief homily at mass. So, in order to preach well, the priest must meditate the Word he preaches. He must place his life under the Word so that he can proclaim it authentically. So there is a continuous circle between preaching, prayer and preaching. In other words, the priest must open his life each day to the experience of God. Rahner has said that the Christian of tomorrow must be a mystic or he will be no Christian at all. This is even more true of the priest. Although Rahner recognizes that it is a bold affirmation and although he is aware of his own spiritual poverty, he dares to say that a priest must be a man who has an experience of God. People today are searching for God and they turn to priests expecting that they have such an experience of God. So the priest must be one who dares to open himself each day in faith and trust to the unfathomable Mystery who grounds his life. He must not be afraid to surrender himself into the darkness of this Mystery, trusting in Christ who walked this way before him.

The Evangelical Counsels

On the one hand the consecrated life is self-evident for the Church. Under various forms it has existed from the beginning. The heart of it would seem to be virginity and the renunciation of marriage, which we find in Paul (see 1 Cor. 7). Certainly after the age of the martyrs, virginity became the normative form of the testimony of self-sacrifice proclaimed in the gospel.

At the same time, Rahner recognizes that the evangelical counsels are anything but self-evident. In what sense is it legitimate to reject human values such as marriage, autonomy, the use of the world's goods? Certainly, if we are going to renounce an earthly good, we must do so in the name of a higher good.

Rahner argues that the meaning of the evangelical counsels becomes evident only if we return to the Christian experience of God. As we saw earlier in our study, God is always the God beyond the world. God is the transcendent. Hence no value within the world can ever satisfy us. We are made for God. This truth is at the heart of the gospel. Jesus lives for his Father. He preaches a Kingdom which is not of this world (a Kingdom which of course impinges on this world). It is this faith of Jesus which allows him to face his death in sovereign freedom. He trusts in the God who is beyond the world to save him. This the Father does in the resurrection. As followers of Jesus we hope for the glorification of our bodies beyond the grave. To use the technical language of theology, our hope is eschatological , that is, not for this world but for the world to come. Only in this context can something like a vow of virginity make sense.

Another way of putting this is that Christian existence is always a share in the cross of Christ. Christ dies to everything of this world. In death he entered into the void or abyss where all disappeared and only trust in his Father was left. Each of us by our baptism pledges to walk with Jesus along this way. All Christian life in this sense involves death to self, or perhaps better death to selfishness. That is why St. Paul says we must use the things of this world as though we did not use them, those who are married for example as though they were not, those who mourn as though they were not mourning (cf. 1 Cor. 7:29-31). The ultimate test of our participation in the cross of Christ will be the death which inevitably each of us must face. Will we in that moment be able to let go and place our hope in Christ alone and in his Father?

The person who takes religious vows anticipates death through the renunciation of precious worldly values. All this only makes sense if he or she hopes beyond this world and trusts in the victory of Christ's cross. Otherwise the sacrifice of the vows is masochistic denial of the beauty of life and of God's creation. We must never forget that the vows are the free renunciation of that which is good.

As I said above, every Christian life must express this transcendent hope and trust in Christ's cross. In whatever profession we exercise, in whatever friendship, in the beauty of sexuality expressed in marriage, our hope must ultimately be in God alone. Consecrated life in the Church is a special witness insofar as its very form gives concrete expression to the Christian's final hope based on the cross. As Rahner puts it, "The evangelical counsels constitute an objectivation and a manifestation of faith in that grace of God which belongs to the realm beyond this present world. And this objectivation and manifestation precisely as such are not achieved in any other way of life."[1] Certainly there is no guarantee that a religious is more holy than a lay Christian or a married one. But the Church needs this form of life as an unambiguous testimony of her faith in the fact that the fashion of this world is passing away and our ultimate home lies in the mansions of our heavenly Father.

Christian Marriage

In Rahner's reflections on Christian marriage he develops the point of view he has worked out regarding the nature of the sacraments and applies this to matrimony. At the same time he applies his understanding of grace.

In looking at grace we have seen how our relationship with the transcendent God, although immediate, always has an earthly mediation. We noted as well that these mediations are not merely natural. When I love my neighbor, this love is sustained by God's love. Hence the love of neighbor is not just an ethically good act but deserves the name of charity. In this sense the exclusive and selfless love of a man and a woman in marriage is the supreme example of charity. Something analogous could be said of any genuine friendship.

Moreover Rahner notes that marriage has a paradoxical structure. At first sight it seems to be exclusive. A man or a woman freely chooses a spouse. One

---

[1] K. Rahner, "On the Evangelical Counsels, <u>Theological Investigations</u> 8 (London: Darton, Longman and Todd, 1971), pp. 160-161.

is chosen to the exclusion of all the others. But in fact this seeming exclusivity is deceptive. First of all, the marriage union opens up to a third, the presence of the child, the fruit of their union. If the two decided to remain closed in on themselves, their marriage would be a form of egoism. Any true love opens out, it bears within itself a fruitfulness. Further reflection reveals that indeed the family can only exist within the wider framework of society in general, and ultimately in the context of the whole human family. In fact all human beings are bound to one another. No one exists in isolation.

If we put together what we have said thus far, we see that marriage is a reflection of grace, that is, the union of God and humanity. Moreover, we see that any given marriage reaches out in a certain sense to all of humanity. Thus, in this perspective, we see that marriage is an anticipation of the union of God and humanity which comes to its fulfilment in Christ. In fact in the Old Testament, God's relationship to his people was seen as a covenant (see, for example, Ez. 37:26). Indeed this covenant was likened to a marriage bond (Is. 62:4). In the New Testament, the union of God and humanity is likened to a wedding banquet (Mt. 22:1-14). Christ himself is called the bridegroom (Mk. 2:19). And in Ephesians, chapter 5, marriage is seen as the great analogy of Christ's relation to the Church (Eph. 5:32). The faithfulness and the selflessness of the love of husband and wife reflect the faithfulness and love of Christ and his Church.

In his treatment of the sacraments Rahner has shown that in the sacraments Christ's victorious love becomes visible in the world. When two baptized persons love each other and seal their love in a public covenant, it is clear that Christ's love is becoming transparent in the world. In a sacrament Christ offers an infallible pledge of his love to a person in a concrete situation, that is, in a critical moment of his human history. If this is the case, it is not a surprise that marriage is a sacrament. Marriage makes great demands but it is ultimately a gift. The gift of Christ's grace makes it possible for a human couple to be faithful in spite of human weakness. Christ's grace is given to sustain them.

In number 11 of Lumen Gentium, The Constitution on the Church, the Second Vatican Council spoke of the family as the domestic church. This is not just a pretty metaphor. Rahner says that it is literally true. When a family lives together in harmony and peace, there the grace of God is being triumphant in this world. There Christ is becoming visible. There in fact is the foundation of what we call Church, "the sacrament of the intimate union with God, and of the unity of all mankind." (Lumen Gentium, 1)

We might ask what is the situation of the marriage of two non-baptized persons. Rahner argues that we cannot call this a sacrament, for a specific reference to Christ is missing. There is missing the foundation of baptism, where a person explicitly undertakes to walk the way of Christ and to enter into his death and resurrection. So in the case of the non-baptized, there is not the infallible pledge of grace given by Christ to his Church. But Rahner equally argues that it would be a mistake to see such a marriage as graceless. Indeed it is not just natural. For as we have seen, grace is everywhere at work in the world, and so wherever human beings love one another, there is an implicit Christological reference and charity is present. So even a non-Christian marriage is and should be full of grace.

Conclusion

I hope that we have been able to see in this section how the various Christian vocations reflect the fundamental tension in all life in the Spirit. On the one hand, the Spirit always leads us to the ever greater God, the God beyond the world. Hence the Spirit is seen at work in the consecrated life and in priestly celibacy. But at the same time the Spirit always leads us back to the world. Christ sends us in mission. This is seen in priestly ministry and in the witness of married life. God is beyond the world and in the world. The various Christian vocations give concrete expression to this tension.

For Further Reading:

Karl Rahner, "Priestly Existence," Theological Investigations 3, London, 1967, pp. 239-262.

Karl Rahner, "The Spirituality of the Priest in the Light of his Office, Theological Investigations, 19, London, 1984, pp. 117-138.

Karl Rahner, "Marriage as a Sacrament," Theological Investigations 10, London, 1973, pp. 199-221.

CHAPTER TEN

The Role of Mary and the Saint

Growing up in Southern Germany, Karl Rahner was used to great devotion to the saints. The area of his youth, Baden in southern Germany, was noted for its processions, for its celebration of saints' feast days and for its Marian piety. Marian shrines were numerous. It was also a culture that venerated the dead. The people cultivated the graves of their loved ones and All Saints Day and All Souls Day were important religious and secular feasts.

At the same time, as secularism became more widespread, devotion to the saints underwent a crisis. Rahner asked whether people still felt bound to their dead and whether they still prayed to the saints. He was also aware that modern Germany was living in a time when God seemed removed from daily life. God was no longer obvious. God seemed far away and silent.

On the one hand Rahner could accept the silence of God. As we have seen earlier, he felt at home with the God of Mystery. He dared to surrender himself into God's hands. He was prepared to enter into the apophatic mystical tradition where the nameless God was adored in silent wonder.

But Rahner knew that worshipping the Infinite God was not enough to do justice to Christianity. Precisely the challenge of the Incarnation was to find God in history, in the humanity of Jesus Christ. So he felt continually challenged to return to the finiteness of creation and seek God's presence there. He knew in faith that God wished to be found in space and time, in the humanity of Jesus. So he continually tried to keep the balance between the Infinite God and his historical mediation in Christ. Our way into God was Christ's human life. God, having taken on flesh never left this flesh behind. God must always be sought in this history. This history would be valid as our access to God for all eternity.

But there is more. In the gospels Christ identifies himself with the neighbor. He tells us that his face is hidden under that of our brother and sister in need. Whatever we do to the least of his brethren, we do to him. (Mt. 25:40) So not only may we not abandon history in our search for God. We may not abandon either the history of suffering humanity. Faith challenges us to find Christ in the face of our neighbor.

With these basic insights, Rahner can easily understand the communion of saints. Who are the saints but human beings who are our neighbor? All human beings live together in solidarity and this solidarity holds true not only on earth but also beyond death. So therefore it is legitimate to pray for the dead. This is part of my concrete love of my dear ones. And in the same way it is part of the love of neighbor to pray to the saints and to venerate them, for they too are my neighbor. They exist in solidarity with us. We venerate them for they have gone ahead of us on life's pilgrimage and have arrived at the goal of life. They pray for us who are still on the journey. So, for Rahner, even in this special epoch of God's hiddenness, it is altogether legitimate, if not always easy, to stay in contact with the saints. In fact the communion, which we have with the saints, is nothing other than the living out of Christ's commandment to love our neighbor.

All of what we said just now applies to Mary, as the most pre-eminent among the saints, but Rahner develops his understanding of Mary in far greater depth because of her special place in the economy of salvation. To understand Rahner's Mariology, let us go back to a few key insights which we have seen in earlier chapters. First, in our treatment of Jesus Christ, we saw how for Rahner Christ is the presence of the Infinite God in history. Christ is God's sacramental presence in the human story. But we also saw that for Rahner human beings are prepared to accept Christ through the working of the Holy Spirit, that is, through grace. Moreover, Christ completes his work by pouring out his Holy Spirit on creatures. God wishes to come to dwell in each human being. The human being is through grace the event of God's loving self-communication. What happens in Christ by the Incarnation happens in us by grace.

These principles provide the foundation for Rahner's devotion to Mary[1]. In short, Mary is the creature most fully redeemed. Mary is the human person in whom God's work finds its perfect response. Mary is a creature. She stands wholly on the side of the creature, in contrast to Christ who is both divine and human.

---

[1] For a short but penetrating overview of Rahner's theology of Mary, see Mary, Mother of the Lord, Theological Meditations (New York: Herder and Herder, 1963).

Mary is in no way worthy of adoration, but in Mary we do see the goal of all God's dealings with human beings. She is full of grace, she is the tabernacle of God's presence. She points to the goal of God's saving activity for all human beings, to be the dwelling place of God in Christ.

For Rahner, as for most Christian theologians, the center of devotion to Mary is her divine maternity. Mary is the Mother of God. This is the reason for her greatness, this unique role which she played in the saving history of God. But Mary's maternity is not first or even primarily a biological maternity. Her maternity is linked to faith. God does not force human beings to accept a mission, rather God invites them. So God invited Mary to respond in faith to his plan to send his Son to humankind and Mary responded with her yes of faith. As the Fathers of the Church stressed, she conceived Christ in her heart by faith before she conceived him biologically in her womb. This yes of faith is the source of her greatness.

So we see Mary as the archetype of true humanity. She says yes to God and so she becomes full of grace. Christ chooses to live in her. And Rahner notes that in her yes, there come together the two dimensions of mission and person. As persons each of us is unique. God has a unique project for each of us. We realize ourselves by accepting this project which God offers us in love. Mary fulfilled herself as a person by accepting her unique mission. Something similar must happen for each of us.

Here once again we see a link with Ignatian spirituality. In the Spiritual Exercises Ignatius presupposes that the retreatant will make an election. He will choose a state of life. But this election will be made possible by God's grace. God will show him the choice which God wants, the choice offered in love by God as God's way of fulfilling the person. Rahner always insists that God's project for us cannot be derived by abstract principles, by reason alone. We know God's project by opening our hearts to God in prayer where we wait for God to reveal his preferences. All this for Rahner is most beautifully exemplified in Mary's response to her divine mission.

Mary is venerated as the Mother of God, but there is another dimension which is important for her role in the economy of salvation. Mary is the Virgin Mother of God. As we read so clearly in the gospels of Matthew and Luke, Mary conceives Christ without the aid of a human father. She conceives him virginally. Once again Mary's virginity is not of interest primarily from a biological point of view. Her virginity has to be understood in faith. In what sense then is virginity an important symbol of faith? Here we must be careful. We cannot as Christians denigrate the body or sexuality. Whatever is created by God is good. Mary's virginity is an exceptional gift and has value precisely because it points to the fecundity of God's grace. Before God, and especially before our need of God and God's salvation, we creatures can only stand empty. We have no claim on God. We are completely unable to do anything to establish union with God. This human incapacity is symbolized in virginity. As a virgin Mary cannot give birth to God's Son. But all things are possible with God. (Lk. 1:37) So Mary's virginity and virginal conception symbolizes both human incapacity and divine omnipotence.

Rahner says there are two great symbols in the history of salvation that express fundamental human attitudes to God. One is the tower of Babel. Humanity by its own resources wants to reach up to heaven and grasp the divinity. The other symbol is the virgin from Nazareth, who places her empty womb before God in an attitude of faith and waits for God to make her fruitful by giving birth to his Son.

If Mary's whole personhood is assumed into her mission, then, according to Rahner, we have a key for interpreting the doctrine of the Immaculate Conception. This doctrine wants to say that God's grace has been effective in Mary from the first moment of her existence. From all eternity Mary was thought of with a particular mission, namely that of becoming the Mother of God. Mary's role was indispensable in God's becoming Incarnate. Therefore Mary needed to be prepared for her mission. God prepared Mary's fiat, her yes, by enveloping her life with grace from the beginning.

This doctrine regarding Mary was not clear from the earliest moments of the Church's life. It was a conviction that grew as the Church meditated on the mystery of Mary's role in salvation history over the centuries. Even in the thirteenth century St. Thomas refused to teach it and it was strongly rejected by the Reformers such as Luther and Calvin. Their reason for rejecting the doctrine was Paul's teaching about the universality of sin. For Paul, in Adam all sinned. (Rom 5:12) Therefore all needed the grace of the Redeemer. Although Catholics maintain that Mary was sinless, they also maintain that she was redeemed by Christ. In fact, the grace of the Immaculate

Conception was a special privilege granted to Mary in virtue of the merits of Christ won for humanity on the cross. Rahner's teaching on Mary fits into this perspective. Mary is the most perfectly redeemed. She is free from sin not by her merits but uniquely through the grace of Christ. In our case Christ's death has freed us from our sins. In Mary's case Christ's death has preserved her from sin. But in either case Christ alone is the Saviour and Redeemer.

Looking at Mary as the most perfectly redeemed also gives Rahner a key for interpreting her assumption into heaven. What is the redeemed human being like? We must obviously look to Christ. As God incarnate, Christ fully embraced our flesh. He in no way despised the body but became bodily, and that not just for his earthly pilgrimage but for all eternity. The risen Christ lives in the glory of his Father in his glorified body. So that becomes our hope as Christians. We profess our faith in the resurrection of the body. The goal of human life is not just the immortality of the soul beyond death but life in the flesh before God. In the unforgettable setting of Handel's Messiah, we remember the words of Job, "I know that my redeemer liveth and in my flesh I shall see God." (Job 19:25).

If this is our Christian hope, then it makes sense to affirm that Mary already lives in God's Kingdom with her glorified Son and she does so in both body and soul. She has already reached the goal of the human journey. As the most perfectly redeemed, she lives the glory of Christ's resurrection. Obviously this is a privilege for Mary, but still there is a link between what happened to her and what we hope for for ourselves. What Mary has achieved remains for us the goal of our hope. Here again we see how Rahner links grace and anthropology. Mary possesses the fullness of grace. But the grace is given to her not just for her sake but for ours. Where she has gone, we are destined to follow.

What we have just said prepares for the final point of Rahner's reflection on Mary. Mary's graces are not just for herself but for us. For her mission is to be the mother of all believers. We spoke in the beginning of this chapter about the communion of saints, about the solidarity of all believers in the communion of saints. Mary too exists in this solidarity. Indeed she is the foremost member of the communion of saints. If we venerate the saints and if we trust that they are praying for us, this is even more true of Mary. In this sense Rahner is prepared to accept the notion that Mary is the mediatrix of all graces, certainly not in the sense that Christ is the Mediator. Christ is Mediator in a unique way. He is both God and man and stands on both sides of the divide. Mary is only human, but as human, and as perfectly redeemed, she is bound to us in solidarity. She intercedes for us. It is Rahner's conviction that Mary's role in heaven reflects her role on earth. Her yes to God's plan was a yes that embraced all of humanity. God intended all to be included in the Incarnation, as Jesus was to be the first of many brethren (Rom 8: 28). So in heaven Mary continues the work of intercession, and the scope of her intercessory power is without limits. From heaven she looks upon humanity with compassion and desires that all be caught up in the love of her Son. Her mantle is spread wide to embrace all and we can trust in her maternal love to protect us so that we arrive at last with all the saints in the Kingdom of her Son.

For Further Reading:

Karl Rahner, <u>Mary, Mother of the Lord</u>, Herder, 1963.

Karl Rahner, "Why and How Can We Venerate the Saints," <u>Theological Investigations</u> 8, London, 1971, pp. 3-23.

Celebrating the Liturgical Year

In this chapter let us look a bit at Rahner the preacher. Throughout his life Rahner always understood himself as first and foremost a Jesuit priest. He didn't set out to be a great theologian. He set out to be a priest. He was convinced that at heart he was an "Ordensmann", that is, a follower of his religious congregation, the Society of Jesus.[1] As such over the years he gave constant sermons and spiritual meditations. In this chapter we pursue some of the insights of his meditations into the great Christian mysteries. For it is in celebrating these mysteries that God's Spirit touches us in the here and now.

Christmas

Walter Kasper once remarked that faith in Jesus is like an ellipse with two foci. One is the Incarnation and the other is the paschal mystery. Following this insight, I will here seek to show how Rahner's spiritual meditations revolved around these two great foci of faith.

Rahner's introduction to the theology of Christmas at first struck me as very strange. He exhorts us: if we

---

[1] Rahner often stressed this point in interviews in his latter years. His life, he said, had been nothing more than that of a typical Jesuit.

want to enter into the spirit of Christmas, we must first have the courage to be alone. Surely this is strange advice. For our culture tells us that Christmas is a time of sharing, a time to be together. But Rahner insists that we will never experience Christmas unless we experience an aloneness.

What happens in this aloneness? Well, Rahner says, we have to endure ourselves. We become aware of our own restlessness, our emptiness. But this can be the first moment of grace. The great Fathers of the Church always insisted that our restlessness is implicitly a searching for God, since God alone can fill up our emptiness. They also taught that we could never search for God, if God had not already found us.

So in our aloneness we might get some taste of God, God the Mystery, God the silent and unmasterable one. And in this silence we can yearn that this God draw near to us. Indeed we might even get some taste that he is close to us.

So this emptiness (Rahner would surely call it a graced emptiness) prepares us for the unimaginable gospel of the Incarnation. God has drawn near to us in the flesh. God has taken on our own humanity, our own history. This is the good news of Christmas. In a striking phrase, Rahner writes, "The experience from within and the message from without come to meet each other."[2] Rahner is here thinking of the silent experience of prayer and hearing the preaching of the gospel. But this phrase in itself sums up Rahner's whole approach to the experience of God as we

[2] Rahner, "Thoughts on the Theology of Christmas," in Theological Investigations 7 (London: Darton, Longman and Todd, 1971), p. 28.

have explored it in previous chapters. All our experience of God comes to us in the depths of our personhood in grace and in our human story through the Incarnation.

So the solitude of prayer, our enduring of ourselves leads us to the Incarnation. And this Mystery is the source of our peace. Christmas is about peace on earth, but not the peace that human beings can create. It is peace bestowed on those on whom God's favor rests (Lk. 2:14). How can we have peace in a world of warfare and bitter divisions? How can we have peace in a heart so restless and threatened by anxiety? Surely only by the Incarnation. For Christ has taken on the entirety of human life. He has experienced in his own flesh all the torments of human living. And he has resolved all those tensions in his living, dying and rising. Christ's human story shows us the way to find peace on our journey. By letting his humanity be the pattern of our own, his peace heals the divisions within us and among us.

Good Friday

In addition to his theological writings on death, Rahner has a number of devotional pieces which treat the question of Good Friday. As usual Rahner's approach is existential. The death of Christ has to be linked to human death. Thus Rahner calls one of his meditations: Behold the man! (Jn. 19:5) Obviously Rahner intends here the Christ of the passion, but he also understands the human being faced with his own death. For Rahner, like Christ, the human being is stretched out both horizontally and vertically. He is stretched out horizontally in history. His life comes out of his past and is projected into the future. At the same time, there is a vertical dimension to human life. The human being is suspended between heaven and earth. He is an openness to God. Living between the horizontal and the vertical, the human being experiences his finitude. And the supreme sign of this finitude is death.

For Rahner the most important thing about Christ's death is that he has accepted our common human lot. He fully experienced the death of man. And Rahner stresses that he was neither play-acting nor pretending. He simply died the death of man. At the same time Christ's death is not heroic. Christ is not a superman. Rather he is God truly in the flesh. Rahner stresses the adage of the Church Fathers: "All that was received and accepted has been redeemed."[3] In particular Rahner points to two aspects of the death of Christ as seen in the Scriptures. One is how death threatens us with meaninglessness, the failure of all our human projects. Like us Christ looks into this abyss: "My God, my God why have you abandoned me?" (Mk. 15:34) But at the same time Christ points us to the faith dimension of death. In the midst of this failure and collapse, in the midst of the seeming futility of it all, Christ cries out, "Into your hands I commend my spirit." (Lk. 23:46) So Christ shows us the possibility of a death in faith.

Holy Saturday

One of the things which is striking about Holy Saturday is that it is a day in between. Nothing hap-

---

[3] Rahner, "See, What a Man!" in <u>Theological Investigations</u> 7, p. 138.

pens on Holy Saturday. It is a day of waiting, a day of silence. Rahner notes that it is a non liturgical day. There is no Eucharist on Holy Saturday.

In one of his meditations on Holy Saturday Rahner notes that the doctrine of the descent into hell is traditionally associated with Holy Saturday. In this doctrine which we proclaim in the Creed, the Church has affirmed two things. First, Christ really died. Secondly, Christ liberated the souls of the just. The Eastern Church traditionally stresses the latter point and sees Christ's descent among the dead as a triumphal journey.

Rahner rather stresses the first aspect. On Holy Saturday Christ is really dead. We saw in our previous chapter that for Rahner death is both active and passive. There is the act of dying in which we surrender ourselves to God. But there is also the passivity of death. We are helpless and powerless. Only God can save us from death. So Rahner stresses that Christ really suffered this powerlessness. In his human nature he needed to be redeemed from death by his heavenly Father. This passivity of death involves another dimension as well. In death our spirit is separated from our flesh. Our body in its totality dies. So we are no longer worldly, fleshly. Rahner stresses that this is something unnatural. God has created us as embodied spirit, this is what God wants us to be. In this sense death is unnatural. And Christ has so fully identified with us that he suffers that state of 'unnaturalness'. He too is without his flesh. He must await the resurrection of Easter Day.

In another essay, Rahner meditating upon Holy Saturday, takes as his theme the saying of St. Paul: Our lives are hidden with Christ in God (Col. 3:3). This is the reality of Holy Saturday. The death of Good Friday has hidden Christ from our eyes. We see only the corpse. We do not see the living power of the eternal Son. This will be revealed on Easter.

Here once again Rahner stresses the link between Christ's death and ours. As we have seen, for Rahner death is not just a biological event at the end. We are constantly surrounded by death. It is a constant possibility for us. At any moment we can anticipate our death, this slipping away into nothingness. So at any moment, we are challenged to believe Paul's words, "Our lives are hidden in God." (Col 3:3)

Rahner sees in these words an invitation to the Christian to persevere. Death stands before us, the dark night, into which we must all go, the hiddenness of God. But we do so in faith, clinging to hope in Christ. He too once lay in death. We trust that our Holy Saturday as well will give rise to the dawn of Easter.

Easter

Rahner has written extensively about the Easter mystery. Here I wish to underline a few brief points. First Easter is an absolutely unique event. For Easter doesn't mean that Christ has come back from the dead. Rather it means that he lives, and not just the life of the flesh, but rather Christ lives in the glory of the Father. He has passed beyond this world into the world of God. So the resurrection stands on the boundary of time. We can date it from our point of view with the first witnesses, but with his resurrection Christ bursts out of time into God's eternity.

Like all Christian theologians Rahner stresses that the resurrection is the ground of our Christian faith. Our faith stands or falls with Christ's resurrection. As Paul says, if Christ is not raised, then we are the worst of fools and we are still in our sins. (I Cor 15:17)

Moreover, we have to stand within Easter faith to believe it. It is not possible to prove the resurrection of Christ from the dead. Admittedly we can show that such faith is reasonable. We can point, for example, to the reliability of the witnesses and to the empty tomb. But still to move to faith we need the grace of God. In short only the Holy Spirit of Christ can convince us of the truth of Christ's resurrection.

What we see here is the typical structure of Rahner's approach to God. All our knowledge of God has an historical mediation. The greatest mediation of all is Christ's death and resurrection. And this historical mediation has historical witnesses in the first Apostles. But the historical is never enough. Without grace there is no experience of God.

Speaking of the grace of the resurrection Rahner makes the beautiful point that we experience this grace in our human hope. Each of us hopes for ourselves, we hope for the fullness of life, for a fullness that gives definitive shape to our lives, for a fullness that overcomes all fragmentariness. This is in fact nothing other than hope in life beyond the grave. In this life the reality of our human existence will always be fragmentary. But we hope beyond this for a totality which Rahner calls eternity. Indeed in human life we have moments of flash when we get a glimpse of this, such as when we gather the whole of our lives into a unity when we make a moral decision of great importance. In simple language we hope that one day we will be fully ourselves, fully alive, body and spirit, in a fullness that death cannot touch. Rahner argues that this hope is more than natural. It is a hope planted in us by God's grace. It is this hope, which Rahner calls a graced hope, that gives us the courage to believe in Christ's resurrection. When we hear the good news of Christ's resurrection, grace recognizes what it has been looking for. In this sense Easter is the great feast of hope. We hope that the fullness of life which Christ now possesses with his Father will one day be ours.

Ascension

Rahner makers three points about the Ascension of Christ. First, Christ is no longer with us in the flesh. Second, he will come again just as he was and is. Third, his departure prepares us for his coming in glory.

First, Christ has gone away. This was an incredible shock to the first disciples. They had lived with him, seen him and heard him, even touched him, and they had learned to find in his presence God among them. Christ during his ministry had healed them and taught them the way to God. Now all that was over. So the Ascension brings pain. God Incarnate is no longer visible to us. This makes us sad. It can make us anxious as well, and for that reason Christ in his farewell address prepared the disciples for his departure. "It is good for you that I go away." (Jn. 16:7) Why? First because Christ prepares a place for us and second, because in this way he gives us his Holy Spirit. From henceforth he will be present in every time and in every place, no longer limited by his condition during the years of his earthly ministry. But of course the Ascension challenges us to faith. Rahner calls it the feast of faith as such. Ascension marks the state of humankind from now on until the end. We see Christ not with our physical eyes but with the eyes of faith.

But secondly, Ascension contains the promise that Christ will come again. And not just that. The Christ who will return is the same Christ. He will come just as he was and is. Christ does not leave his body behind nor does he dispose of his human history. This history remains and will remain forever valid as God's presence among us. We wait for no other than the same Jesus of Nazareth who lived two thousand years ago.

Finally, Rahner calls the Ascension the festival of the future of the world. The Ascension points inevitably to the second coming. Meditating upon this Rahner emphasizes the materiality of our faith. God became incarnate in Christ. Christ still retains his flesh. When he comes again, we will be like him. Our bodies will rise and be glorified. So Ascension points to the future transformation of our world. Some evolutionists may believe that our present world may one day take a great leap into a new form of spirit. Rahner says that we are denied any such expectation. God has definitively embraced matter. The future of our world will inevitably be material. It will be nothing less than the glorified humanity of Christ united to the glorified humanity of his saints.

Pentecost

Rahner's meditations on Pentecost revolve around a tension in two Christian texts. First there is the verse of St. John's gospel, where we are told that the Spirit had not yet been given because Jesus had not yet been glorified (Jn. 7:39).And then there is the text of the Nicene Creed which speaks of the Spirit who spoke through the prophets. How can these texts be reconciled? Rahner's heart lies rather with the latter text which sees the Spirit as everywhere at work in the creation and in human history. His perspective as a theologian is clearly a universalist one. But equally he recognizes the definitiveness of the Christ-event. Rahner resolves the tension in this way. From the first moments of history a dialogue was initiated between God and humankind, God always searching for the response of love from his creature. God has never been absent from human history. But this dialogue reached its climax with the Incarnation and the paschal mystery. So from that moment the Spirit found its perfect response. The Spirit has, so to say, become visible in Christ, forever bound to him. And the sign of that indissoluble link is the Church. The Church with its sacraments makes Christ visible in the world. Hence when Peter preaches his first sermon, he tells his hearers that they must repent and be baptized. Response to God must become visible and tangible by accepting Christ and his Church. All grace has an ecclesial direction. Indeed Pentecost is the birthday of the Church.

From this Rahner draws at least two important conclusions for the spiritual life. First, since the dialogue between God and humanity has reached its culmination, every man and woman is confronted with a serious choice, whether to be caught up into the Christ-event or not. The gift of the Spirit on Pentecost brings with it a serious responsibility for human beings: the challenge of belief or unbelief. The second conclusion points in another direction, offering human beings unshakeable trust. In the Incarnation and on the cross God has won a definitive victory. The future of history and of our individual lives is not in doubt. We are destined for eternal life in Christ. Therefore, for the man or woman who believes, there is a sure foundation for trust. "Nothing can separate us from the love of Christ." (Rom. 8:39)

The Eucharist throughout the year

In our reflections thus far we have been meditating upon the great feasts of the Christian cycle. But of course most Christians celebrate the Lord's death and resurrection every Sunday and indeed many Christians celebrate Eucharist daily. How does Rahner understand the significance of this ongoing liturgical prayer? A key theme here for Rahner is everydayness and he insists on the importance of finding God in our everyday activity and of the importance of the Eucharist in helping us to do so. When writing about the everyday, it seems to me that Rahner reflects a certain pessimism, perhaps due to his temperament or perhaps influenced by his culture, growing up on the edge of the Black Forest. Rahner certainly admits that daily life offers its joys and its creativity. But in general Rahner tends to see in everydayness drabness and monotony. I was reminded of the French saying that life is 'boulot, metro, dodo', that is, job, underground and sleep. Certainly Rahner is convinced that every life has its share of frustration, failure, disappointment and sickness. And in all this he sees what he calls, <u>prolixitas mortis</u>, that is, the thread of death.[4]

But if this is the case, the Eucharist does not represent an escape from life. It is true that the Eucharist represents a sacred space where we feel the nearness of God. But it is also true that Eucharist is nothing other than a celebration of the Lord's death and resurrection. We remember in every Eucharist how Christ confronted the failure and abandonment of death and how his faith in God was the source of his triumph over death. So for us too, every Eucharist is an antidote to the death dimension of ordinary life. In the Eucharist we unite our daily lives to Christ and so find the resources to live the triumph of Christ's resurrection in the midst of death.

It is interesting to note here how Rahner admonishes us that if we are to succeed in linking our daily or Sunday Eucharist to our everydayness, we need to 'withdraw into ourselves'. As we saw at the beginning of this chapter, it is exactly this attitude which Rahner recommended for entering into the spirit of Christmas. What he means by this is a certain recollectedness, a certain solitude, in which we have the energy and the courage to confront ourselves and our lives, to face up to the anxiety which everydayness presents to us. Here I think we see more clearly Rahner, the existentialist, Rahner the former student of Heidegger. Heidegger in his early writing had spoken of the everyday man, the average man (*das*

---

[4] With this phrase Rahner is referring to a sermon of Gregory the Great. See "The Eucharist and Our Daily Lives," in <u>Theological Investigations</u> 7, p. 218.

man) as the one who is only too ready to flee into triviality, to lose himself in the morning's newspaper, the addiction of football, the latest soap opera or the gossip of the local pub and so avoid the challenge of living authentically. For Rahner the Eucharist is a daily invitation to authentic living, a daily invitation to look death in all its forms in the face and unite that death to Christ's. But even the Eucharist can only help us to do this if we are ready to accept the solitude which lets Christ's grace work in us. But if we do this, we are promised that we can share not only in Christ's abandonment in death but also in his resurrection into eternal glory.

For Further Reading:

Karl Rahner, "Thoughts on the Theology of Christmas," Theological Investigations 3, London, 1974, pp. 24-34.

Karl Rahner, "He Descended into Hell," Theological Investigations 7, London, 1971, pp. 145-150.

Karl Rahner, "On the Spirituality of Easter Faith," Theological Investigations 17, London, 1981, pp. 8-15.

Karl Rahner, "The Church as the Subject of the Sending of the Spirit," Theological Investigations 7, London, 1971, pp. 186-192.

Faith, Hope and Love

In this chapter I propose to look at the so-called theological virtues of faith, hope and love. These virtues have been a classical theme of theology throughout the centuries. They are called theological virtues because they have God as their object. By living these three virtues Christians claim that they have an experience of God. Let us see how Rahner understands this claim.

Faith

On a number of occasions Rahner said that we live in a wintry time for the Church and for faith. Even when Rahner was a child, faith was practically taken for granted in his culture. As he grew older, faith no longer formed an obvious part of culture. The language of faith was perceived by many people as strange. God didn't form an obvious part of the landscape of culture.

Rahner also noted that many people have a distorted idea of God. In the past, even the recent past, God was seen as a law-giver. God gave the commandments telling people how to live. Not bowing to this God of judgment carried the threat of eternal punishment. The Church had the role to propose a rigorous morality. Church and state worked together to enforce traditional moral values.

119

Today men and women live in a secular culture. Ours is a world where empiricism and functionality reign. The prevailing language is that of the computer. Reality is often measured by the stock exchange. The world market is perhaps the overarching story which rules our culture.

In one sense Rahner's whole theological project is meant to call men and women back from losing themselves in objects to discovering themselves as mystery. Human life is mystery open to the ever-greater Mystery of God. In this his thought has parallels with the philosopher, Martin Heidegger, who saw human beings as dragged into a preoccupation with beings like persons swept under water by an undertow. Heidegger wanted to summon them to Being. Rahner gives a theological interpretation to this modern human experience, exhorting his fellow human beings to return to the mystical dimension of life, that is, to surrender to God the unfathomable depth and ground of our being.

As we saw in the chapter on God, for Rahner God is the incomprehensible whom we can never master with our intellects. However we can surrender to him in trust. This then is the meaning of faith. In the midst of this world's preoccupations and occupations, in the midst of life's joys and sorrows, in the midst of the darkness of suffering and death, we can dare to surrender ourselves into the hands of the living God. In this we follow Christ, who likewise lived the reality of faith even to the point of drinking the bitter dregs of death on the cross.

In this way Rahner rejects a utilitarian view of religion. God is not useful (we cannot use him to serve our purposes) and precisely in this way he is more than useful. For he is the ultimate depth of our life.

I already stressed in chapter two that with this vision, which I believe is at the heart of all Rahner's theological writings, there is a reprise of the classical mystical tradition. Rahner stands in the great tradition of mystics such as Teresa of Avila with her famous adage: 'God alone is enough', in the tradition of St. Ignatius Loyola with his fervent prayer: 'only your grace and your love, these are enough for me', in the tradition of the anonymous author of the Cloud of Unknowing who invites us to penetrate this cloud of darkness with the dart of love.

Hope

During the 1960's there was a great resurgence of thinking about hope. Partially this was due to the optimism of that decade. In America, the time of President John Kennedy seemed to open a new era of hope, so much so that his time was referred to as Camelot. In Europe it was a time when there emerged in philosophy a strain of humanistic Marxism. Marxism always had an orientation to the future, toward the time of the classless society. Many commentators saw in Marxism a form of secularized Judaism. Humanity like the Jewish people of old was marching to the future of the Messiah.

One thinker who wrote significantly about hope was Ernst Bloch. Bloch, a secular Jew, wrote three volumes entitled, The Principle Hope. Bloch presented a vision of utopia. He took the word utopia in its literal sense (i.e. 'no place'), humankind was moving into an empty space where the new man was to be born.

This idealized humanity did not exist as yet, it was in the process of being born. In a famous phrase, Bloch reversed the old Aristotelian idea that the subject is identical with the predicate in truth (for example, the sky is blue), and said rather that the subject is not yet the predicate. S is not yet P. That is, 'man' does not yet exist. However it is this open space, the future, that draws matter forward until one day the new humanity will be born. Whereas in Judaism the future was to be given by God, in Bloch's philosophy, God did not exist. Rather there was the empty space where one day would be 'man'.

Rahner wrote numerous articles on hope and various articles on the relationship between Christianity and Marxism. In his great synthesis, <u>Foundations of Christian Faith</u>, Rahner offered a short summary of faith in terms of hope. He affirmed that Christianity keeps the question of the human being's absolute future open. Indeed this absolute future is God. But as we have seen throughout, God for Rahner is the fullness of Mystery, here seen under the angle of hope. The human person is moving into an ever greater fullness whom we call God, and moreover this God draws near to us in grace and in his Son Jesus Christ. Believing in Christ gives us solid grounds to hope that our future is not death or nothingness, but rather the fullness of the unfathomable Mystery.

Here Rahner is obviously picking up the emphasis in contemporary philosophy on the human being as historical. For philosophers such as Heidegger, history is not something out there, but rather a dimension of human being. Indeed the primary category for the human is the future. This is what makes the human being human. He or she is not an object but rather freedom, freedom as openness to an indeterminate future, freedom as the ability to project oneself. Rahner builds on all this, interpreting human freedom precisely as the openness to God, God not seen as static Omnipresence but rather as the Absolute Future drawing the human being forward. Yet this drawing forward is not into emptiness, for in Christ human beings have learned that this future is love, love which has drawn near in graciousness.

Not only did Rahner speak of God as the Absolute Future but he also specifically reflected on the fact that hope is a theological virtue and he asked himself why. As we have seen throughout, Rahner never left his roots in the philosophy of St. Thomas Aquinas. Aquinas spoke of the human being as having the two spiritual faculties of intellect and will. Rahner did not speak of faculties, but he always saw the human being under the dimensions of knowledge and love. It was easy for him to link these two human acts to God. Christianity had always referred to the second person of the Trinity as the Logos or Word. The Word was God's self-expression. Human beings know God in his Word through his Revelation. But the New Testament also speaks of God as love, because God gives Himself away. This dimension of God can be linked to freedom. St Augustine in fact linked the two processions of the Trinity, the emanation of the Logos and the Spirit to the mind's knowing itself and loving itself. So Rahner can see clearly why there is the theological virtue of faith and that of charity. Faith is linked to belief in the Logos and charity to the outpouring of the Holy Spirit. But why is hope part of the triad? Why is hope the third theological virtue?

Rahner's answer is brilliant and absolutely consistent with his central vision of God. God is the ever greater Mystery. In this sense God remains always unmasterable and unavailable. We can never control God. This is true not only in this life but also in eternity. We should not think that by seeing God in the beatific vision we will understand him. On the contrary we will know ever more clearly that we can never fully fathom God. We will be blinded by God's dazzling light. This means that in our relationship to God we must always trust. We must project ourselves into God, the ever greater Mystery. For all eternity we will be invited to make that surrender. And this is the meaning of hope. We project ourselves into God's future, allowing him to master us, and that not just on earth but in heaven.

Rahner makes another point as well. With faith we believe in God's revelation. So we believe that God wills that all be saved. That is fine and important. But how do we make the transition from the general truth to a conviction that God wills me to be saved? Rahner once again answers through hope. By hope I make the link between the general truths of Christian faith and their truth for me. I dare to trust that I will be saved because of my Christian hope. Hope is the link between the general and the particular. To put it in the more technical language of theology, faith allows me to believe that God's grace will be sufficient for all. But through hope I come to grasp God's grace as efficacious. I dare to trust that it will be effective in my life. Hope brings in the very personal dimension of faith. It believes that God's will is gracious not only in general but for me. In this way Rahner sees hope as a kind of bridge between faith and love. Hope makes God's love concrete for me and pushes me to surrender to it in love.

Perhaps much of what Rahner has to say here is abstract and may seem remote. Does our human hope have anything to do with daily life? Is this hope in God's Absolute Future just pie in the sky? Rahner makes the obvious point that hope must become concrete in our daily lives together especially in the life of society. The Second Vatican Council said that our hope for the next world does not lessen our efforts in this life but rather reinforces them.[1] Our ultimate hope is a stimulus to create here and now parables of the Kingdom, to create a life on earth which foreshadows that of the Kingdom to come.

In writing on hope, Rahner also affirmed this point. He suggested that we have two types of hope, the major hope in God's Kingdom, in God as Absolute Future, the future which we can never fully realize in history. But equally we have minor hopes based on this major hope. These minor hopes are seen in the concrete human projects which we seek to realize on the basis of the conviction that God has drawn near to us in love and that Christ has died for all. If Christ has died for all our brothers and sisters, then surely this fact must stir up in us a sense of solidarity,

[1] The Pastoral Constitution on the Church in the Modern World affirms: "Therefore, while we are warned that it profits a man nothing if he gain the whole world and lose himself, the expectation of a new earth must not weaken but rather stimulate our concern for cultivating this one. For here grows the body of a new human family, a body which even now is able to give some kind of foreshadowing of the new age." (no. 39).

a desire to do all in our power to alleviate human suffering and injustice and to anticipate in so far as possible God's Kingdom of peace and righteousness. In this sense Rahner says that Christianity is anything but a conservative religion. In principle, as the religion of hope, it is never on the side of the status quo but on the side of the revolutionary. Genuine Christianity will always be a catalyst for the new. Christian hope will always inspire believers to take risks for a more authentic humanity. Risk rather than paralysis is the characteristic note of Christian hope.

Charity

St. Paul tells us in his Letter to the Romans that "the love of God has been poured into our hearts by the Holy Spirit who has been given to us." (5:5) So we have God's own love dwelling within us. As we have seen in chapter three, this love has been called grace in the theological tradition. By the grace of the Holy Spirit we participate in the divine life.

But Rahner also poses a further question. What is the relationship between the love of God and the love of neighbor? He wants to insist on a radical unity and see these two loves not as just two things juxtaposed. For Rahner when I truly love my neighbor, I am in fact also loving God and God's love is dwelling within me.

Rahner notes that there are a number of biblical hints which point in this direction. For example, St. Paul says that love fulfils the whole law (Rom 13:8) Then in Matthew's gospel, there is the scene of the last judgment, where those who are saved are told that whenever they did these things to the least of

Christ's brethren, they did them to Christ himself. (Matt. 25:40) So here we see a Christological identification between Christ and our neighbor in need. Thus the New Testament affirms that we will be judged on our acts of charity: feeding the hungry, clothing the naked, welcoming the stranger etc.

Rahner also recalls the theological tradition about a morally good act. If a person is in the state of grace, a morally good act is judged to be more than natural. It is in fact supernatural. That is, it is borne by the grace of God. This is why our morally good acts are efficacious for our salvation. And Rahner argues that this is true as well for the anonymous Christian, that is, the good man who does not know Christ explicitly, but who lives according to his values. The Catholic Church teaches that all persons of good will can be saved. But one can be saved only if one has charity. Where is such charity seen in the lives of anonymous Christians? Rahner answers precisely in their love of neighbor, in their selflessly good moral acts.

Rahner also appeals to his philosophical understanding of human transcendence. As we have seen, human beings perform acts of knowing and loving. In knowing, the subject and the object are one in the act of knowing. But a human being not only knows. The human being also disposes of himself. The human person makes himself through the actualization of his freedom. Freedom always presupposes an otherness. I make myself in relation to the other. But no material other can ever complete me, precisely because I am also more than material. I am a subject, a self-presence, with an infinite interior depth which makes me mystery. So if I am ever going to realize myself in freedom, it will have to be by giving myself away to another person, to a Thou.

Pursuing this reflection further, we note that human transcendence never stops at the finite other. As we have seen from the beginning of this study, transcendence is dynamic and orients us to God. Thus if I can ultimately realize myself in freedom by giving myself away to another, finally that other must be God, the infinite source and condition of possibility of my freedom. Already in our chapter on God, we saw how Rahner affirmed that genuine freedom ultimately means surrender to God. But here we need to stress as well, that this freedom for God is always mediated through the human Thou. There is no direct access to God which bypasses the human. So I surrender myself to God, by giving myself away to my neighbor.

Of course the deepest reason why this is true is because of Christ. He is the concrete human being who is the Mediator between God and humanity. Rahner argues that all love of neighbor is implicitly a searching love for Christ, that finite reality who is also Infinite because He is the divine Person in the flesh. Human experience reveals that it is possible to love my neighbor with a certain absoluteness. For example, a man pledges himself unconditionally in marriage to his wife. A mother loves her child unconditionally. It is even possible for a man to love his friend unconditionally, for example, caring for him in an illness to the last moment. But how can we explain that absoluteness in the contingency of a human relationship? Rahner argues that we explain it through the God-man. Every person in loving his neighbor absolutely is looking for God's absolute love in the flesh, that is, Jesus Christ.

So Rahner argues that the love of God and the love of neighbor are not two loves but one. In and through my neighbor, I am loving nothing less than God himself, mediated to me in space and time.

For Further Reading:

Karl Rahner, "Brief Creedal Statements," in <u>Foundations of Christian Faith</u>, london, 1978, pp. 448-459.

Karl Rahner, "Reflections on the Unity of the Love of Neighbor and the Love of God," <u>Theological Investigations</u> 6, London, 1969, pp. 231-239.

Karl Rahner, "On the Theology of Hope," <u>Theological Investigations</u> 10, London, 1973, pp. 242-259.

Conclusion

Finding God in the World

Throughout these pages we have sought to develop the idea that Rahner is an Ignatian theologian. Ignatius of Loyola has been his key inspiration. In following Ignatius, he has presented a vision of how every man and woman can have an immediate experience of God, and that not by a mysticism of flight from the world but by finding God in the world.

However, throughout Rahner's writings, he has sought to maintain a clear dialectic. He has interpreted Ignatius as first and foremost a monk, a Christian therefore who places the love of God above all things, who recognizes that God is utterly transcendent, who cannot be captured by worldly realities. In this sense, a monk who wishes to be crucified with Christ in the world, who places all his hope in the resurrection from the dead and hence on the Kingdom of the world to come. In Rahnerian language, God is the Holy Mystery, unfathomable, unavailable, the Infinite Ground of all that is.

But precisely because this God is infinitely free and not bound by any creature, God can give himself to creatures in the Holy Spirit. God is free to become flesh in Jesus Christ. God is so transcendently free that he can be found wherever he gives himself. As we saw in the chapter on Ignatian discernment, both Ignatius and Rahner offer criteria as to how we can discover God's presence in the world.

And so Christian spirituality is a dialectic between the God beyond and the God who is near, between the Transcendent God and the God in the World. In this way Rahner challenges us, like Ignatius, to be able to say that we have had an experience of God in our lives, in our human histories. And this not because of some natural mysticism where we discover God in the stillness of solitude or in the beauty of a sunset, but rather because we have found the Holy Spirit of Jesus operating in our lives, bestowing on us peace and joy in the midst of life's challenges and struggles, in the midst of work, family and relationships.

So Christian life in the Spirit presupposes a dialectic of two virtues: first a holy indifference or inner freedom whereby we are not tied to any creature because we know that God is greater than all creatures and at the same time a willingness to give ourselves heart and soul to human projects, for we know that God can inspire us to do this and to find him in them. As the classical adage of Jesuit spirituality puts it, to trust in God as if everything depends on him but to engage ourselves in the human task as if everything depends on us. The critical point is to maintain a just equilibrium between these two.

Looking Back

As we look back on the journey we have taken together, I believe that we can verify a few key insights and intuitions in Rahner's understanding of life in the Spirit.

First, all of his theology is God-centered. His constant motif is God the Holy Mystery. In a certain sense all of our experience of God will be apophatic, that is nameless and imageless, because God is always the ever-greater.

At the same time God is constantly available to us in human transcendence. In all our knowing and loving, God is present to us as our ground and goal.

If God is always the ever-greater, this fact does not deny that our immediate experience of God constantly requires mediations. In this sense, Rahner maintains, like St. Thomas Aquinas, that we have no experience of God which does not begin in sense experience, in our insertion in the world. If this is true on the basis of creation, it is even more true on the supernatural level. The greatest mediation of all is the Incarnation. For Rahner, as for every Christian, we will always go to God through Jesus Christ. All our prayer, all our action must ultimately have a Christological basis. Even those who do not know Christ explicitly, can only go to God through Christ. In their case, their knowledge of Christ is indirect. It comes insofar as they assimilate themselves to Christ and his values. For those who know Christ 'anonymously' as well as for those who confess him in faith, the neighbor remains the great mediator between God and humanity.

Speaking of mediations, another great theme in Rahner's spirituality is sacramentality. If God is present to us in Christ, then Christ is present to us in the Church. And the Church manifests itself in the seven sacraments. Rahner is convinced in faith that Christ has won the final and decisive victory over sin and death on the cross. This victory will ever shine forth in the world. To guarantee this, Christ leaves us his Church. As Church we have the constant mission to become the light of Christ's victory to the world. We do this especially through our holiness as we live out the vocation which God gives to us according to his unpredictable calls. In this way the Church becomes the communion of saints.

As we just said, Christ is the final mediator. But we should be more precise and say that the ultimate mediation between God and the world is the cross of Christ. Through his Incarnation Christ lived a fully human life. He fully embraced our humanity and so he did not shrink back from experiencing even human death. Christ's life on earth was a life of obedience, of constant surrender to his Father. The ultimate test of this obedience took place in the darkness of Calvary. In the midst of death Christ continued to hope in his God and for this reason the Father raised him from the dead. Ultimately, for Rahner, faith in God stands or falls, with Christ's death. Every day the Christian gospel invites us to stake our all on the cross of Christ. Can we continue to hope, even in our moments of darkness and abandonment, and especially in the ultimate powerlessness of death, that Christ is the victor? This is the challenge of believing in God: daring to surrender all to God with the dying Lord Jesus.

And so we come full circle. God is beyond the world. So we let go. We let go even in death. We let go of everything and let God be God. And yet we know this is ultimately not abandonment. For God has chosen to share our fate. God is with us in Christ, in his life and in his death and resurrection. With Paul, we know: "Whether we live or die, we are the Lord's" (Rom. 14:8). For the God beyond all our words, thoughts, and images is the God of Jesus Christ, who will bear our human flesh for all eternity. In this sense, our world is truly a world of grace.

For Further Reading:

Karl Rahner, "The Ignatian Mysticism of Joy in the World," Theological Investigations 3, London, 1974, pp. 277-293.
Leo O'Donovan (ed.), A World of Grace, New York, 1980.

their appropriate context they exist as mediators for the surrender of our lives to God . . . . Moreover, when distinguishing between Consolation and Desolation, we in essence find that the principal difference lies in whether these motions of the soul enable us to make an act of faith, hope and love or whether they block such virtues. We are not to be naïve in looking at consolation and desolation. The immediate emotion can often be deceptive. It depends on the general condition of our souls: in the terminology of the Spiritual Exercises, whether we find our-selves in the first week or the second week. For example, a person beginning the Exercises and in need of conversion may be filled with repugnance at leading a moral life. The values of Christ might seem demanding even overwhelming. So he needs to resist, regardless of discouragement. But the situation is different for a man in the second week. If his heart is firmly rooted in Christ then he should nor-mally experience peace and joy, the fruits which St. Paul associates with the Spirit (see Galatians 5.22-23). So in this case, consolation involves positive emo-tions whereas discouragement would be seen as the work of the evil spirit. One sees here that the trajec-tories of the first and second weeks are contrary. The type of "delight" experienced in the first week, for example in sensuality, is the "work of the Evil One," whereas delight in the Second Week will be the work of the Holy Spirit.

In a short essay in America magazine,* William Barry suggests that a fundamental rule of thumb is to

* See the issue for July 30, 2012, pp. 13-15

Further Bibliographical References:

Burke, P. Reinterpreting Rahner, A Critical Study of His Major Themes, New York, 2002.

Dych, W. Karl Rahner, London, 2000.

Endean, P. Karl Rahner and Ignatian Spirituality, Oxford, 2001.

Lennan, R. The Ecclesiology of Karl Rahner, Oxford, 1995.

McCool, G. The Rahner Reader, London, 1975 (introduction especially useful)

McDermott, J.M., "The Christologies of Karl Rahner," Gregorianum 67 (1986), pp. 87-123, 297-327.

O'Donnell, J. The Mystery of the Triune God, London, 1988. (chapter 2 on Revelation and Trinity with reference to Rahner)

O'Donnell, "The Concept of Mystery in the Theology of Karl Rahner," Heythrop Journal XXV, 1984, pp. 301-318.

Sesboué, B. Karl Rahner, Paris, 2001. (French)

Williams, R. "Balthasar and Rahner," in John Riches (ed.), The Analogy of Beauty, Edinburgh, 1986, pp. 11-34.

Finito di stampare
nel mese di Marzo 2004

presso la tipografia
"Giovanni Olivieri" di E. Montefoschi
00187 Roma • Via dell'Archetto, 10, 11, 12
Tel. 06 6792327 • E-mail: tip.olivieri@libero.it

always possible to experience God, that we are called to an immediate experience of God in everyday life. At the same time Rahner doesn't deny that there are specially privileged moments where God's presence is felt more vividly. These experiences are not totally different from other experiences of God but they are heightened experiences of grace. Other theologians have spoken of disclosure experiences or signals of transcendence; Rahner thinks along the same lines arguing that there are privileged moments in which one has a heightened experience of grace. Examples would be: courage in the face of death, hope in a situation where there is no tangible motive for hope (for example in a concentration camp), love of another human being without any search for human compensation, fidelity to another without any reserve, willingness to forgive another gratuitously, an ultimate confidence and trust in the value and meaningfulness of human life, an implicit sense of being accepted, an ultimate felt reality. If fundamentally attentive to these and other similar experiences, human beings experience the gracious and loving reality of God in sheer immediacy.

For Further Reading:

Karl Rahner, "Reflections on the Experience of Grace", Theological Investigations 3, 1974, pp. 86-90.

Karl Rahner, "Man as the Event of God's Free and Forgiving Self-Communication", Foundations of Christian Faith, London, 1978, pp. 116-137.